MW01697460

The Mexican Mix

a memoir

Patricia Rodriguez

with David Rodriguez

Copyright © 2019 by Patricia Rodriguez

All rights reserved. No part of this publication may be reproduced, distributed, or transmitted in any form or by any means, including photocopying, recording, digital scanning, or other electronic or mechanical methods, without the prior written permission of the publisher, except in the case of brief quotations embodied in critical reviews and certain other noncommercial uses permitted by copyright law. For permission requests, please email prod1939@aol.com.

Cover and interior design by Tabitha Lahr

Published 2019
Printed in the United States of America
ISBN: 978-0-578-59535-1
E-ISBN: 978-0-578-59536-8
Library of Congress Control Number: 2019916874

For permissions questions, contact prod1939@aol.com.

I dedicate this book to my son, David, a gifted author, who wrote on his cell phone, in one month's time, his autobiography, *When the Lights Go Out*, bringing the reader with him on his adventurous life as a boxer, winner of six championship belts, survivor of a violent attempted murder on his life by knife, world traveler, sports commentator, public speaker, and champion of bullied and hospitalized children. He also once saved my life and inspired me to write.

Contents

Part I: David

Chapter 1: From Michigan to Mexico 9
Chapter 2: A Different World Awaits 13
Chapter 3: Graciously Consumed by Family. 22
Chapter 4: Getting America Back 28
Chapter 5: Juárez Cantinas to Mexico City 34
Chapter 6: Indio and Cuervo 40
Chapter 7: Reclaiming America and WWII. 45

Part II: Patricia

Chapter 8: Another Kid's War Years. 61
Chapter 9: From Roof Jumping to Chest Thumping . . . 72

Part III: David

Chapter 10: Racing to Adulthood—Grabbing the Reins. 81
Chapter 11: Salvation or Annihilation 89
Chapter 12: A Batman Day 95
Chapter 13: LA, Gypsies, Heists, Slim Living 99
Chapter 14: Solidly A Sailor 108
Chapter 15: Naval Leave: Juárez to Vallejo 117
Chapter 16: Kobe, Japan—Aika's Bar, Big Mac's End. 122
Chapter 17: Back to Mexico. 129

Chapter 18: A Stake in America—Now A Cop 136
Chapter 19: Death at A '50s Drive-In 143
Chapter 20: A Shot in the Face 147
Chapter 21: Reconnecting and Disconnecting 154
Chapter 22: A Fist to the Face and One to the Gut . . . 167
Chapter 23: Now A Detective 176

Part IV: David and Patricia

Chapter 24: Life and Love Tsunami 183
Chapter 25: Inescapable Descent into Racism 194
Chapter 26: Being A Private Eye 198
Chapter 27: The Finishing Line, The Starting Line. . . . 207
Chapter 28: Whipping Out Swim Laps 215
Chapter 29: Grabbing the World 220
Chapter 30: If You Want to See Old Mexico 228
Chapter 31: Silk, Slugger, Spice, Sad 241
Chapter 32: The Big Bang of Mexico. 259
Chapter 33: The Nightlife 262
Chapter 34: All Shades of Fun 265
Chapter 35: An Economic Jolt on Both Borders 271

Epilogue: Winding Down and Exploding—
Quick Exits 279
Through a Mother's Eyes 284

Part I: David

CHAPTER 1

From Michigan to Mexico

I ANGRILY PULLED MY squad car over to the curb and leaped out, leaving the door swinging open to find its own way to closing, trying to escape the soaked crotch and shirt of my uniform, which was making my skin crawl. I had once held a partner in my arms as his head wound spewed gushing blood over me, and I felt only the agony of his pain, but this dousing in body fluids nauseated and greatly annoyed me.

The call I had just answered was to assist a woman who had just crossed the border from Juárez into El Paso and was in critical and imminent stages of labor—in need of assistance. I had arrived at the street corner to which I was directed to assist her and helped her into my squad car, where she'd sprawled out on the back seat and opened her legs, screaming. She was in the last, and severely painful, stage of delivery.

I'd called for an ambulance and leaned into her as she clutched my arm, yelling "ayudame"—"help me." Her water, mixed with blood, broke right into my face, upper body, and crotch area. I grabbed the exiting baby and wrapped it in an available towel I happened to have in the squad car. As the woman screamed frantically, I made a call for immediate help and then occupied myself with trying to make sure the baby didn't die.

When the ambulance swept her and her baby off, I was left with a stench-soaked uniform and a feeling of anger that this woman had imposed such trauma and danger on herself and her baby just to ensure its birth took place on the US side of the border, giving it automatic US citizenship. She had crossed the bridge into the US from Juárez after her labor began, waddling in the last stage, and called the El Paso Police to send help once she was safely in the US.

I didn't sign up for this crap.

As soon as I left the birthing scene, I headed for the closest refuge, which was my parents' home in central El Paso. As I climbed the old cement, slightly crumbled steps, I thought about how I had done the same thing all my life. After excursions to Mexico and my naval career throughout Asia, I was back once again. I had done a loop around the world and come back to the same chair. Chasing down all the ventures my mind had conjured up over twenty-six years of my life had left me at this doorstep again, now as a cop.

Four years earlier, this job had gripped me with intrigue and challenge. Now, though, years of rotating eight-hour shifts monthly from daytime, to evening/early morning, to full night hours made any scheduled daytime endeavor impossible to adhere to, and any sleep schedule erratic. This life was both mentally and physically disrupting and disorientating. I was winding down in commitment.

I had transitioned from running the streets as a kid to patrolling, picking up kids for things I had done myself with my young friends, many of whom were now doing prison time for advancing to serious crime. One of my longtime friends had attempted a bank robbery and killed a guard, for which insanity he'd gotten thirty years in Leavenworth; countless others had spent their young years skirting the law with minor crimes like theft, assault, and battery and were now uselessly meandering through their twenties, destroying their lives instead of building them.

I knew my stint in the Navy had saved me from the same aimless existence. For the past few years, policework had done so as well—but now it was bringing the same restless agitation that had led me to leave the military. I knew I would move on, but my still-active imagination could not yet supply an answer or path for the next venture.

This dilemma had brought me to reflect on my extensive family ties to World War II and the recent Mexican Revolution, which had entangled and entwined my mother's and father's lives and produced me, a half-slice of each, with the percussions of both phenomena ingrained in my soul and mind as a "just yesterday" happening. I was scorched by the prejudice heaped on my Mexican dad, but enhanced by the Mexican culture in which he had immersed me.

As I stepped through the fractured front screen door, I saw my mom, Gracie, seated at the table, quietly gazing at that familiar old picture of herself with her father, Lloyd. She rarely took out the old photo, taken when she was eleven years old in her Detroit, Michigan childhood home, or even mentioned her father. When she did speak of him, however, it was with great admiration and almost sacred reverence. I knew the history.

I was there to clean up. I went straight to a bedroom and changed my uniform to a fresh one I had left in reserve at my parents' house, and then came back and sat down at the table that had been a staple of my childhood.

"My father, Lloyd, was great by all measures," my mother said, still staring at the photo. "He was a doctor who had just returned from the First World War. He was strikingly handsome, with an imposing six-foot-four frame and impressive strength. There was a magnetic pull of his personality, and the way, when he walked into a room, his presence was felt by all commanding attention without effort."

I said nothing, just let her speak. I wanted to hear everything I could about this grandfather I never got to meet.

My mother smiled a little. "His stamina, the very force of life within him, gave off vibrations that were infectious to all." Then, flatly and without expression, she said, "There was never any explanation to me why he shut the door to his study one day when I was a little girl and shot himself in the head." She gazed blankly at the photo. "My daddy just left my life. My daddy left me to dream of him, and to dream him into a god and an idol."

She continued in a kind of detached tone of voice, looking away from me. "As I grew older, I realized in my soul that he had made the actual choice to leave me, and sometimes my thoughts of him were with a cold heart, but always that drive to be around him that I had known since I was a baby, and that secure happiness his presence had given me, emerged to the surface, and once again, he was the greatest, most fantastic man who ever lived."

From here, my mother continued her story. I could not extract myself, but soon I didn't want to; I was compelled and mesmerized as the history of my family came to greet me.

CHAPTER 2

A Different World Awaits

AT NINETEEN YEARS OF age, my mother, Gracie, was sick of living with one relative after another, which had been her life since her father's death. She had also met my dad, Jesus Rodriguez, a young man from Mexico. Joe, as she had Americanized him, was handsome and quiet. He was twenty-nine, well-seasoned through a hard life, a hard worker, and seemed to have a stable future with Ford Motor Company in Detroit, which had hired him on his arrival from Mexico two years earlier.

As she listened to him talk about his life in Mexico, Gracie knew he was a man who could take care of her anywhere. Pancho Villa, he told her, had been in a real rage when Francisco Madera, his beloved friend and the president of Mexico, was murdered by General Victoriano Huerta in 1913. Then the Revolution really got terrible. Villa's revolutionaries all over Mexico harassed Huerta's regime. Joe told Gracie he was a young adult when he realized the *Federales* and revolutionaries were both evil. He took her back with him, through his memories, to his village of Uruapan, as he recounted to her in descriptive detail the life-changing Revolution that demolished cities and villages as it marched through his country.

"My village was dusty and quiet," Joe reminisced. "There were no trucks or cars then, only mules to carry the goods. One day, I was standing barefoot on the warm *caliche*, using one hand to finish off a corn *tamale* and the other to hitch the mule. Three *Federales* came into the village on horses, looking tired and worn. They seemed to be just travelers passing through, not posing any threat. After they had drunk from the well and filled themselves on beans and tortillas through the hospitality of the women, they began to call for everyone to gather for an announcement. They waited while the men came in from their cattle to join the women and the barefoot children around the well. Then one spoke in a loud voice, saying, 'We are here to tell you the state of Mexico, your country. There are evil forces attacking your government, trying to demolish it, and with it your whole country. These traitors are everywhere. They are armed and hide in the cities, the mountains, the small villages. There are said to be revolutionaries here in your village.' He paused and looked over the small audience of frightened villagers, all of whom stood mute and expressionless, trying to avoid any interaction with the *soldado* who was speaking in an increasingly menacing tone. 'Whoever joins the revolutionaries or gives food to them will be shot.' Two village men began to back off very slowly, looking for a way to disengage. They were looking on passively and did not know their lives were in danger, but they knew to keep quiet, to show no expression. The one was smoking a cigarrillo, the other holding a child tugging at his serape.

The *Federale* who spoke locked his eyes on them, called to them, 'Don't you believe what I'm saying is true?' One of the men answered in a low but firm voice, 'Yes jefe, but we have no interest in such things.' The *Federale* growled, 'Then I'll show you all to have an interest.' He pulled the two men to the center of the well; the man with the child let her slide down from him to run to her mother. The *Federale* shot the men in the stomach, leaving them to suffer much agony before dying. 'Now,' he informed the villagers, 'you will all have an interest.'"

Gracie listened quietly, horrified by the violence of the story.

Joe continued in a mournful but matter-of-fact tone, "I had seen men hurt, I had seen a man break his leg and sweat for days with the pain, I had seen old people and many children die with sicknesses, but I had never seen such screaming agony as these men with their intestines laid open."

Gracie grimaced but didn't speak. She knew her father was a hero who'd fought in the First World War, but he never spoke to her about it. He had explained the flu epidemic to her as a future precautionary warning, but this was her first awareness of the turmoil in Mexico during the same period. She was engrossed in Joe's story, but with an edge of foreboding.

"To leave the village was dangerous; the revolutionaries would kidnap you and make you join them. And the lifespan of revolutionaries was short, for they died of gangrene from bullet or knife wounds, or swiftly in battles with the *Federales*. To stay in the village was dangerous, too, however, as the *Federales* or revolutionaries would come and shoot you, accusing you of taking their enemies' side. I knew I soon had to leave." He shook his head. "I had been in the village school six-and-a-half days a week for ten years, but the revolution had cut my schooling short. Los Hermanos Maristas, the French and Italian brothers who taught the older children, were being murdered and run out of Mexico by the government, on the pretext that they were thieves."

Joe became more reminiscent as he spoke. "The United States was involved in its own war—the First World War. Although disruption was pervading every Mexican township, my brothers and I had established a whiskey producing business. Especially in those turbulent times, whiskey was in high demand and our business was thriving and well known in our area. A group of industrial Mexican businessmen approached me and my brothers and said they would finance the trip to Detroit, Michigan for us if we enrolled in the Ford School of Technology, which would train us in the field of auto mechanics, and take that knowledge back to Mexico to enhance the businessmen's automotive venture." He smiled. "Our escape had been handed to us. I traveled with two of my brothers; we left the Revolution and the *Federales* behind. I was luckier than most of the migrants who flocked out of Mexico to the US to take jobs during that time—typically exploitive low-wage work offered to eager, hungry, and desperate people fleeing the destitution and havoc of the Revolution. I was welcomed and accepted by the Ford School. I completed my program within two years and then was employed there by the Ford School."

Gracie was compelled. She listened attentively, encouraging Joe to tell more of this Mexican history of which she'd never been aware. "And you've been here ever since?"

Joe shook his head. "The First World War's end brought many layoffs and the Spanish Flu Pandemic of 1918, which for four years continued to scourge the whole world. Thousands of people died, and in the States, people lived in terror. There was no cure for this plague. Some of the strong survived it, but youth or strength didn't ensure immunity. The movies and pool halls were closed as people were discouraged from gathering in groups of more than four. The dead were being buried so fast, in order to cut down on contamination, that there were horrifying rumors that some poor souls were even buried alive." His face was grim. "The Flu Pandemic ensnared one of my two brothers who had gone to America with me. The virus could be stealthy or swift in delivering death, so my two brothers and I made our way back to Mexico on a banana boat to escape further exposure to the deadly illness. We knew our family plantations would offer safer refuge and medical care, as one of our uncles was a doctor."

Gracie's eyes widened. "Did he survive?"

"Yes," Joe said, "but he and my other brother never returned to America. I was determined to reinvest myself into the American economy, though, so I returned to reestablish my life here. My desire was to successfully immerse into American culture. Returning to the Mexico of my youth had brought me dismal memories of why I had left—the poverty and the still dictatorial nature of the government. I established myself as a permanent American resident, but never gave up my Mexican citizenship, nor did I attempt to acquire American citizenship."

And now Joe had gotten a transfer back to Mexico through his job. The excitement of leaving her current life and moving to an entirely new country made Gracie anxious and thrilled. Together, she and Joe left the frozen city of Detroit, Michigan, for Mexico City.

It was a good time to leave for Mexico. The Revolution there was over, and the fear among the people had subsided. Life again was relatively tranquil and simple, and Joe wanted to get back to his people, to introduce his new bride to the warm, hospitable culture of his homeland. They left for Mexico with buoyant spirits. Gracie was seven months pregnant and spoke not a word of Spanish, but she expected that wonderful adventures lay ahead of her.

The train pulled into Mexico City in the dead of winter. Gracie stepped off the train thinking it was damned near as cold there as it had been in Detroit. Her back was screaming against the rumbling journey and the baby felt as if it had shifted down a couple inches, making her waddle more then walk. At that point she couldn't have cared less about what city she was in; she just wanted to get into a bed as quickly as possible.

They journeyed by horse and buggy across this, one of the largest cities in the world. Through the lumpy, chilling ride, Gracie was impressed by little except the startling, obvious contrast of wealth and comfort against the background of half frozen, ill-clad beggars. Even three- and four-year-old children walked the freezing streets barefoot, kind of in a daze, begging for coins.

What happens when they get sick? she wondered. *I suppose they just get well or die.* She shook her head. "Why doesn't Mexico take care of her children?" she asked Joe. "Where are her orphanages?"

"Most of these children have parents who know they are begging," Joe explained. "They are poor and send the children out to collect money. The younger they are, and the more pitiful they look, their chances of a handout are enhanced."

Gracie saw many mothers with a filthy bag on their

arm, dragging a one- or two-year-old behind them, stopping people and asking for some small help.

"Other children are strays though, who have lost contact with their parents and are living off the streets," Joe continued. "Wagons come through the streets daily to pick up the dead of all ages, found in the streets, where they have died in place, or been put onto the street by their relatives without any ceremony after dying. For many of these people, a funeral is simply not affordable. This is not so much a choice as it is that they are just desperate and have no means to take care of their sick or their deceased family. They are not bad people, Gracie, just without hope."

Joe explained the Mexican culture as they viewed it up close. Mexican people were prolific, he said, no matter what their income level. Their children were their pride. Destitute women with nine to twelve children were common. They didn't know how to feed them, but they had them. They also didn't know how to stop having them if they wanted, except by the obvious course of abstinence. They were victims of their husband's desire, with no right of refusal.

When Gracie had spent more time in Mexico, she found that the upper class, the five percent, carried off Mexican culture and tradition with fine elegance. There was nowhere to be found more graciousness or refinement than among a Mexican family of quality. Their manners were impeccable, their hospitality warm and abundant. Their palatial homes reflected the best purchases from Europe and the constant labors of the servant class, who polished, cleaned, and obeyed for a few pennies, or even just for food.

This extended back to 1517, when Hernán Cortés landed on the Mexican peninsula, conquered the Aztec empire, and claimed Mexico for Spain. The Spanish settlers who invaded and possessed Mexico established a culture of Spanish blood superiority; they firmly believed in their God-ordained right to exploit and keep subservient the mixed-blood (Indian and Spanish), and especially pure Indian, population. The two-caste system of separating people by their racial makeup resulted in inviolate, distinct assignments of people's access to wealth, education, medical care, and acceptance into social classes. Persons of "lesser" blood could not move into the affluent upper economic level.

That's what the Revolution was all about: seizing power and remedying the grossly uneven distribution of land and wealth in Mexico. But to date, not much change had occurred. Although the Revolution had established a constitutional republic, the Spaniards still remained in possession and power of the seat of the president and elected representatives. Mostly, money had just changed hands. The ruling class, upon the Revolution's demise, stripped priests and nuns of their right to wear their garb in public and cancelled the Catholic Church's claim to inherit land upon the death of the owner, thus allowing the governing elite to acquire the land for themselves instead. Their power base had been enhanced and remained intact.

The peasants, meanwhile, were tired of the Revolution. Those who had supported the revolutionaries had seen no change in their well-being, just death and misery. They'd seen the power change hands many times and to them, all those in power were *banditos*. They couldn't bring themselves to care anymore. Nothing would change. The beggars begged and had babies, and the rural people worked their small *ranchos*, took care of their goats and their few cattle, if they were so fortunate to own some, and lived clean lives, according to their religion and custom of hard work.

This was the Mexico into which Gracie stepped at the end of her long journey from Detroit to Mexico City.

Gracie was stunned by the contrast between what she saw and the romanticism of what she had imagined. She could see the haggard exhaustion of the street peasants and just hoped the future Joe had promised her was still waiting. He had waxed long about the beauty of Mexico, its music, food, hospitable culture and strong family centered communities. He had never addressed the economic squalor.

Uncomfortable and tired, she listened with moderate interest now as her husband spoke as a tour guide. Another time she might have been intrigued, but right now she had a burden of her own: cramps, made worse by the constant jogging of the carriage. She could not spread herself so thin as to be concerned about these aliens who could not get their lives together. She began to suspect, inspecting the passing surroundings, that she might have some trouble in that area herself.

CHAPTER 3

Graciously Consumed by Family

JOE'S MOTHER AND SISTER met them at the small apartment door. They were a kissing clan, Gracie discovered, as was the Mexican tradition. Each person had to be kissed on each cheek and back and forth. They were also superbly gracious, rattling off Spanish without stopping. Gracie understood none of the words, but she could tell they were trying to make her feel at home and were genuinely concerned about the journey's effect on the child she was carrying.

Having a baby in Mexico, Joe had told her before their arrival, was a woman's primary business and the very first order of the day for a new bride. If she waited too long after marriage to announce an impending birth, being over a few months, she was looked upon as a woman with a real problem. A girl child would be acceptable, but a boy child would cause a real occasion to celebrate, for a boy child fulfills a man's ego. Every man should produce a son. Five sons were better. The man who produced only daughters was looked at a bit askance, like he lacked the power.

The bed finally came, and the hot tea, and the foot rub, and Gracie relaxed. The cramps had gone away. She looked at her new family, with whom she would live, and she felt warm, recapturing some of the excitement she had lost on the grueling trip. She would learn to speak Spanish, she decided—she had always been quick to learn. She was pleased that she had married a Latin lover. As soon as this baby was born, she would get into shape and put on some form-fitting clothes that made Joe take notice, and she would go all over Mexico City with her new husband. His mother and sister seemed to have nothing on their mind but babies. They would love to babysit.

The next few weeks went by slowly and became progressively more boring. Joe was at work all day, and at night Gracie would listen to the family speaking Spanish to each other and to friends, with Joe interpreting only occasionally. Living in the small apartment was hard, and she was to learn that life in all of Mexico was hard. They had to bring water into the apartment in jugs and to buy their supply of food daily because there were no refrigerators. She also got sick of beans: beans fried, beans refried, beans on tortillas, beans in a bowl.

Her in-laws were so polite and gracious, they drove her crazy. They kissed her too much, and she was so big now she could hardly move. There was nowhere in the apartment to move to anyway, with its two little bedrooms, kitchen, and something that passed for a parlor that could fit only one old sofa. She still couldn't even understand what they were saying on the radio most of the time, and she didn't get to bathe often enough. It was a ludicrous ordeal to fill up that small tub with water and try to squeeze her big belly into it. Then she could hardly get out again. She was scared about having the baby there in the apartment.

"Why can't I go to the hospital?" she demanded of Joe one evening.

"No one goes to the hospital here unless they're planning on dying," he told her. "Everyone has their babies at home. Besides, we don't have the money."

"I'm scared," Gracie said.

Joe covered her hand with his. "I hired a registered nurse for you, remember? She's ready to come over as soon as you go into labor."

Even that was exceptional for the times, Gracie knew. Here, most babies came into the world at the hands of an aunt or neighbor. She tried to stay positive, and hope for the best.

Gracie had her show of blood at ten o'clock one drafty, cold morning, and her mother-in-law promptly put her to bed, where she had been spending most of her time anyway. She waited anxiously through the day for something to happen, but nothing did, not even a cramp.

Joe came home from work late in the evening and, knowing that this was the night, sat on the bed by her and talked calmly to her of many things. Eventually, they dozed off.

Gracie awoke at two in the morning to a sharp pain. Within less than an hour her pains became more intense, even violent. After another hour passed, she was screaming at Joe to go get the nurse.

"I can't stand the pain!" she cried. "Get the nurse, Joe. I can't stand it."

Joe's mother and sister leaned over her and tried to reassure her in Spanish.

She grabbed their hands. "Please do something," she begged them. "Help me, please!"

She had lost all rationality. She was an animal having a baby.

When the nurse finally came—to Gracie, it seemed like forever—she said it would be a while, maybe a long while . . . some women went twenty to twenty-two hours with their first baby.

In the ensuing hours, Gracie became delirious, as if in another world, consumed with pain. She was nothing but pain.

And then the greatest pain, pain that could not be endured, produced a girl child.

Joe's mother set to work cleaning her up. His sister cleaned the baby. Gracie was limp and still a little delirious and feeling angry. She didn't even care to look at the baby. She had been hurt, she had been through hell, and it was somebody's fault. *It never would have been like this in Detroit*, she thought. Her mother would have seen that she had a doctor and something for the pain. It was Joe's fault for bringing her to this stupid country of backward people.

I'm getting out of here as soon as I can—away from the Spanish and beans and carrying water, she decided.

She drifted to sleep angry.

Joe's mother repeatedly said Gracie would feel better in a couple of days, but in a couple of days she felt worse. An infection had set in and a fever had come.

She had pain in her abdomen and lay in a sweat for days. She worried about the baby, who always cried and whom she could not nurse because she had no milk and she was too sick to move.

For a month, Joe took the baby three times a day to a wet nurse. For a month, Gracie lay desperately sick, fighting the infection with her own body power and medicine that didn't seem to help. For a month, the baby cried.

Then the baby didn't cry as much. She was getting weak. Joe took her four times a day to the wet nurse, but she didn't drink her fill. She was sick with a fever and sores that covered her body. Her little frame was too small to fight back.

For another week, Gracie and her child struggled to stay in the world. Then, finally, Gracie improved until she was almost well, and able to fret hysterically over her baby.

One night a doctor paid a visit to the baby. After examining her, he sighed.

"Nothing seems to help," he said. "I'm afraid the little child will not be alive in the morning. She is expiring before my eyes."

With that, he left.

Only then did Joe finally consent to let his mother and sister apply the folk remedies they'd been pleading him to try on the baby. They ground up tomatoes and a variety of cactus and other plants into a fine mush, following old Indian practice, and applied it to the baby's entire body.

The next morning, the baby was still with them, so they applied the salve again, and again after that, until the baby cried and showed signs of life and hunger.

The danger was over.

Over the next few months, Gracie watched as her baby grew fat and healthy. When they both were strong, she and her girl child left Mexico.

It was in Gracie's strength and nature to overcome this experience, to even make light of it later—or at least to relegate it to a position of little significance in her life. But it was not in her nature to make herself available for it to happen again.

CHAPTER 4

Getting America Back

THE RETURN TO AMERICA wasn't easy. Only youth and passion can fuel the dynamic turnover of one's life and security that is plunging into the unknown with a little baby in tow—and Gracie didn't go back to what she knew, Detroit. Instead, she went to Arizona, where she had an aunt she could stay with as she worked out her future. Joe followed and took a job in the copper mines.

They were off to a hard restart. Joe struggled at the laborious work in the mines. When, after two years, Gracie became pregnant again, he left the mines and took the family to Los Angeles, where he worked in restaurants as a cook specializing in pancakes. The work garnered him enough money to support his small family on a subsistence level, and he often brought home ample leftovers.

Then Joe's brothers in Mexico contacted him, proposing that he start a fruit and vegetable business in El Paso, Texas. There, he would be close to the Mexican-American border, and they could supply him with the ample produce they grew on their massive farms and ranches.

So Joe, knowing his brothers wouldn't let him down, moved with his family to El Paso. There, in a city with a presence of Mexican nationals and Mexican Americans, which gave him a familiar culture in which to be comfortable and with which to do business, he laid down the future of his livelihood.

Gracie loved El Paso's climate, with its decided absence of ice and snow, and her friendly nature adapted quickly to the gracious southwestern hospitality.

She also soon utilized the abundance of low-wage Mexican house maids and general laborers available in the city: for a pittance, a maid would "live in," meaning they would work six days a week, sleeping in their employer's house and performing all housekeeping, cooking, and child-rearing duties. This left them only one day or a day and a night off to return to their home in Juárez or to a safe house in El Paso where they paid a minimal amount to a hostess to have shelter and freedom from work for a night.

Many of the available laborers and maids were from the interior of Mexico and came to a relative or another Mexican acquaintance's home in El Paso to stay, as the hostess would provide them with temporary overnight cover until they were placed, at the discretion of the hostess, with a family seeking a domestic worker, referred to as a maid. The low cost of living was enhanced by having access to Juárez markets, which were a short streetcar ride from downtown El Paso over the border to Juarez. All a person had to do to find a maid was ask around among friends, and someone would have a quick referral; young women from Mexico seeking domestic work in El Paso were plentiful. The preferred maids were from the agricultural part of Mexico, because they were from poor and honest people who were accustomed to hard work, were religious, and were seen as trustworthy.

This abundance of low-cost maids allowed families of lower and middle income in El Paso to have access to round-the-clock maid service ordinarily reserved for only the wealthy. The freedom this allowed women in these households was enhanced by the streetcars that passed hourly between El Paso and Juarez, offering El Pasoans inexpensive shopping alternatives. Gracie felt a power of purchase and a life bereft of laborious housecleaning and cooking that she never would have had access to in her cold hometown of Detroit. She was comfortable taking their small family to Juárez often for inexpensive dinners, to buy goods from street vendors, and to enjoy the blaring Mariachi music. And the children loved riding the open streetcars.

Joe was running his fruit business, and it was rapidly expanding, not only supplying the many Juárez restaurants with the Mexican produce his brothers sent to him, but also selling into Colorado and other Southwest venues.

He made frequent visits to do business in Juarez, weekly and sometimes daily. The extreme poverty he saw daily infused him with the incentive to be successful in his stake in America.

A scrawny dog sniffed furtively around the corner of the open vegetable stand, hoping to uncover a scrap. A large desert roach lay on its back behind the wooden cartons that held mounds of chilies and vegetables. The same fruits that fed the people by day gave a banquet to the insects and roaches that swarmed over the produce at night like a pulsating blanket.

A greasy-haired, dirtily clad vendor raised his hand and a sharp voice at a barefoot four-year-old boy who was fingering the mangos. To men like him, the little street beggars were worse than flies, watching constantly like preying animals, waiting for the vendor to avert his eyes just long enough for them to snatch a fruit.

Joe crossed the dusty street in front of a slowly moving donkey, pulling its daily cart of vegetables and fruit, while the sweaty driver called out to attract buyers. A short Tarahumara Indian squaw with her baby slung onto her back in traditional papoose style approached the cart with a couple pesos in her hand and picked over the produce with painfully slow scrutiny before buying a small handful of fruit.

Juárez reflected the most degenerate sort of life in all of Mexico, Joe thought. Not only were the people poor, they had become street scavengers. At least in the interior, the people lived with their few chickens or goats on small ranchos and kept their tradition of religion and family order. The children worked there with the mother, and the father was the unquestioned head of the family. The air, too, was clean, not like the stink of these streets. The hot months were coming, and these wretched dogs that roamed the streets would become rabid, a constant fear of the peasants who shared the streets with the uncontrolled animal population.

But Joe was doing good business here. His brothers were raising an increasingly expanding crop of chilies and vegetables, and he knew he could extend his market access for them in Juárez and its bordering city, El Paso.

He walked by a café. The hot tortillas being pounded out by the dull-eyed women in the kitchen filled the air outside with a delicious aroma. Well-dressed American tourists were attracted as they passed by and the warm smell of food filled their nostrils. But the dilapidated condition of the café told them they really shouldn't trust it, so they lingered, then walked on to find a cleaner place to eat.

Joe sat at a small wooden table and ate his tortillas covered with heavy chili sauce. Then he crossed the border into El Paso and headed for the hospital. He had to work. He had to keep the family going; otherwise he would sit at that hospital day and night, praying, in agony, for the life of his son.

Three years earlier, Gracie had delivered her fourth baby, a son with a flock of thick blond hair who weighed ten pounds at birth—Gracie said he looked like a Nordic child. A powerful kid with an aggressive personality, he was adored and allowed to do as he pleased. But at the age of three, he fell ill for the first time—with diphtheria.

Every day Joe went and looked through the glass wall separating his desperately ill son—along with the other two hundred sick children in the hospital—from him. Absolutely no contact could be made with him. He watched his tough little son—who was not even screaming furiously anymore, the pain in his throat being too severe to utter a sound—and despaired. Each day another child died.

For forty days, that boy's determined spirit of life fought off death.

Then the pain and fever gradually subsided, giving Joe a surge of hope. Every day began to bring noticeable improvement, so the nurses began to lift him up from his crib and smile encouragingly at his dad, who was staring hungrily through the glass at his treasured son.

After a few more remarkable days, the child was well and screaming for food. Joe got up off the bench in the hospital hall to take the blanketed bundle the nurse handed him. It was the first time he'd touched his son in over a month. The child was still a bit weak and seemed dazed. He looked deeply and blankly into his daddy's face, and then wiggled a hand free from the heavy blankets and touched the familiar mustache. Joe felt a flood of warmth, giving thanks to God at being able to hold this little bundle again.

That was the last sick day ever to touch the boy's life.

As the years passed, people grew accustomed to seeing the blond "gringo" boy keeping pace beside his dark-skinned father, making the rounds in Juárez and El Paso, collecting money for produce delivered and stopping at the corner bar.

CHAPTER 5

Juárez Cantinas to Mexico City

STILL SEATED AT THE table with my mother, relieved to be free of my soaked uniform, I sat quietly as my mom concluded her weaving through our family beginnings. I had begun to remember it from the point when I was a young boy, and to relive with her what I remembered. After I left that day, a flood of my own life memories was ignited and engulfed me erratically for a few days.

The few childhood pictures I have show me to be a blond, curly-haired boy of solid build and strong arms and shoulders. I remembered being joyfully at home in the cantina, singing loudly with the mariachis who strummed their guitars and bellowed sad lyrics of Mexico and love. They wore huge sombreros with their beaded ranch outfits and cowboy boots, and I always managed to get them to lend me one of their sombreros. The giant hat hung off my head and down my back as I perched on the bar stool, sucking down Cokes and occasionally a beer that I saw sitting idly on the bar top. I was a wild kid, never knowing the reins of discipline. I'd bolt off the bar stool and run out onto the dusty street to chase down a donkey cart and ride the donkey's back down the street, yelling with the vendor.

The drivers didn't mind; they were familiar with my stunts.

I spent many days with my dad learning the fruit business, selling and distributing his produce to fruit stands, nightclubs, and restaurants in Juarez, which was profitable. On the American side, I got extra income by selling cantaloupes on the streets, pulling my wagon full of the ripe, ready-to-eat fruit behind my bike until I found a busy corner likely to attract ample and eager customers. On the Mexican side, I knew all the people on the streets—the friendly prostitutes, the bartenders, the cab drivers, the market workers, each of whom was earning a simple living selling their wares or services—and I loved them all. Like my mom and dad, I had an adventurous and amicable nature and loved mingling with crowds of people, no matter their place in the social structure of life. My outlook was realistic: I saw people in their simplest form and found no one offensive. They were all friends. I overlooked weakness, which most people have in some area, and found great humor in human actions of greed or pomposity. I developed an innate understanding of people from this daily and constant exposure to and interaction with the multicultural populations of El Paso and Juarez. I felt comfortable and at home with them all.

On weekends, my mom and dad would take our whole family to Juárez to eat, shop, and listen to the street music. Most of the restaurants we went to also had Mariachis or other live vocal or instrumental music. It became very familiar turf to me. It was fun family time, free from strife. I was very nourished and content with my young boyhood life, especially enjoying the ample time I spent with my dad.

Everything was fun with him, even helping unload and distribute his fruits and vegetables to Juárez establishments and getting my own supply from him to sell on my own. I was out of the house most of the time—if not with my dad, then with friends who ran the streets with me.

Going to school was something that just interrupted my fun. I was more in my element with a loose lifestyle than a rigid schedule requiring studying and being held accountable for teacher-assigned homework. I often didn't even take it home to do, as I had my afterschool fun already planned and it didn't include spending time at a table with books and paper.

My dad loved my company but could see that I wasn't developing the discipline I would need for future success. He had the answer.

My dad always wanted me to know his extended family in Mexico. I was already fluent in Spanish due to his conversing with me in Spanish since I was born, as he considered being bilingual an essential mode of communication in America, especially in the future.

"C'mon David," he said one afternoon, "let's go get my brother from the train."

"Is he my age?" I asked as I ran after him to his old flatbed truck that he used to carry the fruits and vegetables his brothers sent from their huge plantations in Mexico.

My dad chuckled. "No David, he's as old as me."

My interest dissipated as we waited for the train to screech to a halt.

When it did, however, an impressive man emerged wearing a freshly pressed suit, a hat, and an energetic, broad smile. He came down the train steps, his blue eyes focused on my dad and me. He advanced fast toward us and slapped my dad's back, then swooped downward, heaved me up with great strength, and gave me *un abrazo*—a big hug.

I was astonished by my uncle's effusive laughter and commanding personality. He seemed to ignite the air with enthusiasm. He kept his hand on my shoulder and called me "son" as we got into my dad's truck. He didn't talk to me as the seven-year-old kid that I was; instead, he included me in his adult conversation with my dad. I really liked his attention and felt immediately attached to him.

"You keeping the produce moving?" he asked me.

"Yes," I said proudly, "I help unload it and I eat a lot of the fruit."

He laughed heartily.

Uncle Everado stayed with us for a few weeks. At home he always pulled me into the conversation with him and my dad, which made me feel important—especially since my grandmother excluded me from many family activities with my three sisters. It felt good to be pulled in. I spent my time out of school with my dad for that reason, and was delighted to also get a close connection to my newly acquainted uncle. I was really feeling special.

During his visit, we covered the Juárez restaurants and markets we distributed our produce to, ate in Juárez restaurants, saw a few bullfights, and played the gambling machines. Uncle Everado told me long stories about his expansive pottery business on his plantation, and he said I should go to meet his sons and see the beautiful racehorses raised on his plantation.

When my uncle's visit was over and my dad and I took him back to the train to depart, I became suddenly seized with determination to go with him.

"Tío, Tío, take me with you," I cried. "I want to go too!" I pushed toward him and clung to his arm, as I'd gotten used to doing since he'd arrived.

"What do you think?" Uncle Everado asked my dad.

He just shrugged.

Without remorse or falter, I raced in front of my uncle to take a seat on the train.

It was a first-class ride, as were all my uncle's endeavors. At night the Pullman train car had overhead beds, which were very comfortable, and we both had restful nights of sleep. Close to our destination, as we passed through a small town, the train slipped off the track and we had to disembark. My uncle took me to meet his relatives who lived in farming areas nearby. This was confusing for me, as he told me the woman was my aunt and her kids my cousins, but he ignored my query as to who the father was.

As the trip took us closer to his plantation and our trip's end, Uncle Everado took me off the train at two more stops to meet two more fatherless families to which he was very connected—emotionally and also financially, I realized, as he handed each of the women large sums of money. My father later told me this uncle was a compassionate man always helping the poor.

When we boarded the train after each stop, my uncle diverted any boredom he sensed in me by stirring my imagination with wild excitement about the prize at the journey's end: riding the most beautiful black racing horses in Mexico. Whenever he spoke of this, I was swept into the imagery and actual feeling of riding the horses into the wind. I never again heard mention of the relatives we'd met on our trip.

My dad knew this trip would be a learning and growing time for me, a chance to experience the rich culture of Mexico and get to know and love the relatives there that comprised the broad and extended Rodriguez family. Everado had several sons on his plantation; my dad knew I would be well attended and befriended there. Later in my life, I wondered if he hadn't promoted my trip to Mexico with Everado without my being aware that it wasn't solely my idea. I remember clearly how he grinned broadly as the train pulled out of El Paso, carrying me away for my two-year stay in Mexico.

CHAPTER 6

Indio and Cuervo

ENTERING MORELIA, MICHOACÁN, I was astounded at the deep green mountains surrounding the cobblestone streets. Morelia—a city of about 25,000 peasants and their adobe houses, all painted white—gave the impression of a living piece of quaint art in motion.

There, my uncle told me more about the horses on Uncle David's ranch: two black, blazing-fast horses—one named Cuervo, meaning Raven, and the other, which had a perfect white star on his forehead, named Indio. The stories about these speedy, spirited pets of the family, which were used only for pleasure riding, formed fascinating images in my mind. I had never seen a horse except the tired work horses in Juarez, Mexico, who walked with their heads down from dawn to nightfall. The thought of free-spirited horses of the open range soaring into the open wind ignited my imagination, and when we went on to my uncle Everado's ranch, bypassing the horses, I dreamed of them for six months, fantasizing about riding them bareback, in the wild.

When Uncle Everado eventually brought me to Mexico City, I saw through the cab window a city that looked in many areas as destitute as parts of Juárez but also had areas of conspicuous wealth—elegant homes heavily protected from unwanted intrusion by guards and massive prohibitive fencing with huge shards of spiked cut glass on the entire top surfaces of the fences. Mexico City was huge, with a lot of frantic traffic and streets clamoring with intermingling populations of varying incomes—the prosperous and those entrenched in poverty.

In an hour, Uncle Everado delivered me to my uncle Fortunado, who had a house in Mexico City and owned two local drug stores and a ranch located four or five hours out of the city by bus. His home was in Pineland, where his brother, my uncle David, had a house and where the black horses were corralled.

I impatiently waited to see the horses, which were a bus ride and two hours' walk away, neither of which dimmed my excitement.

At last, I saw the horses of my dreams. Indio, the horse with the white patch, captivated me. I wanted to get on his back and ride into the wind immediately. A worker told me that if I'd never ridden a horse before, I should ride Cuervo, as he was the tamest. So Cuervo was saddled and I learned how to use the reins.

Cuervo's ride was easy; after that, I thought I could easily handle Indio. I stayed a week cutting sugar cane with my cousins, and then it was my chance to ride Indio bareback for the ride back to Uncle David's house near the ranch.

I mounted him bareback for an anticipated forty-minute ride, swelling with pride and confidence when the ride started out smoothly. As we neared the house where Indio's stable and food bin were, however, the horse suddenly jerked into high speed and I was forced to hang on by squeezing my legs together and frantically clutching his mane. He continued at breakneck speed for the most terrifying ten minutes of my life.

As Indio ran into the barn, he—purposely, I'm sure—lunged through the door to the barn's food bin with his head lowered so he was clear of the low-positioned door frame, but I was put squarely in the path of being knocked off his back. I ducked my head and body down to hang on his side and gripped his neck tightly to survive the oncoming blow. He stopped short at the feed bin and I quickly slid off, elated to feel the solid ground under my feet.

I thought I would never dream of riding him again. Once was enough.

Years later, though, I would get a quick flash of excitement remembering that feeling of riding into the wind on Indio, the most beautiful horse in Mexico.

My two years of immersion into life in Mexico left me with perspectives of my own history and family relationships that were much more loose and unstructured. I met and loved my uncles and learned the esteem with which their families and all people held them. It was a social structure of male dominance with a place of subordinate but much-loved women, especially my grandmothers and aunts, who shared equal respect but had minimal power to participate in decision making. The man ruled.

I spent a lot of time with three uncles who owned massive beachfront coconut plantations, which established them as wealthy men. Uncle Benjamin had twelve children, Uncle Pepe had two, and Uncle Simon had five. They lived on adjoining properties, so I got to rotate my visits between them. Each uncle had built spacious, elaborately furnished homes of brick or wood. To accommodate the night breezes of the tropical climate, each house had wall sections that could be raised in desirable weather; when that happened, it was like sleeping outside. This pleasure was stifled, however, by the lurking presence of a huge scorpion population for which we had to be constantly on the watch. These creatures measured four to five inches in length, and their attack stance was a raised threatening tail containing life-threatening venom. Our best defense was chickens, which fed voraciously on scorpions, so there were plentiful chickens on the grounds. The women hung large cheese mounds from the rafters of the ceilings near the open beach-view doors to prevent the scorpions' access to them.

One night as I slept with my cousins in a large bedroom, with the wall opening lifted to allow us to enjoy the starlit night and soothing breezes, we all felt a light shower of crumbs from the ceiling. Two huge scorpions had made their way to the cheese and were ravaging it. That brought a quick end to our sleeping under the open night air. We always had to be wary of sitting in areas where scorpions roamed, as one sting would leave a lifetime impression not to be forgotten.

While living in Mexico, I went to a Catholic school where instruction took place in both Spanish and French. I learned to understand a moderate amount of French, and my Spanish became impeccable. I was often complimented as for being a gifted storyteller and speaker, enhanced by the teachers frequently asking me to tell the students stories, some of which were true and some of which I enthusiastically created and delivered with no prior planning. My imagination and delivery were spontaneous, and my listeners seemed to love hearing my stories as much as I loved making them up and spewing them out.

The school also ingrained in me a strong respect for Catholic theology; before returning to El Paso, I made my first communion at the grand cathedral across from the Presidential Palace.

CHAPTER 7

Reclaiming America and WWII

ONE AFTERNOON MY UNCLE Fortunado showed me a telegram he had received from my dad saying that he was sending a close friend to get me and take me by train back to El Paso. I felt joy at knowing I would again be with my dad, but also insecure about leaving the family I had come to love and be very comfortable with. This was a new jolt.

The pickup was swift, so I didn't have time to ponder the future or dwell on the family from which I was being separated. I was returning to America after two years, during which time I'd had no communication with the family I had left there. I was a disciplined, respectful young man, as molded by my Mexican family and school culture, but could now speak only Spanish and no English. I knew I would have to relearn my native language and the customs from which I had been alienated during these years away. I felt I had more structure and security in the Mexican culture, but gradually discarded the strict behavioral customs.

We rode two days and a night on the train, sitting upright, since there was no room to lie down to sleep at night.

My entire family met us as the train pulled into the station. My mother and father effusively lavished hugs on me as my siblings kind of stood back, seemingly wondering where I fit in.

When we reached the house it was a different one than I had left, but it was just as crowded. In my uncle's lavish home in Mexico I'd had my own bedroom, and a modern shower area bigger than the entire one-toilet bathroom of this new house. I immediately wanted my comfort zone in Mexico back. There was little discipline in my family, and noise from kids and dogs was incessant. I glued myself to my dad again and left the house with him the very next day to get to his market.

Another unfamiliar shock to me was the public school I was thrust into after my return. I had been in private school in Mexico, with well-mannered kids, which I had also learned to be. Here I found the same rowdy group into which I'd formerly unthinkingly fit but which now seemed strange. The discipline was not ingratiating or solicitous as it was in Mexico, but rather harsh. A hard ruler whack across the knuckles was the immediate response to any words or action the teachers didn't like. I learned along with the rest of the class to withdraw instead of mingling. I made friends right away, as many of the kids spoke Spanish and my English came back rapidly—but still, I missed Mexico and wondered where I would find my next out.

I found myself again unguided, with no expectation or goals set forth. Thus directionless, I became my own guide to paths unknown. My feelings of estrangement were worsened when I was held back a grade because I was considered language handicapped.

The world of my early childhood now seemed strange and more alienating to me than Mexico had upon my arrival there. My life in El Paso was one of lax discipline, no emphasis on education, no religious practices or instruction—it was a freefall environment in which I had to catch myself. I drifted from religious adherence and expected respect for family members, something that had been strictly enforced in Mexico, into a roaming-the-neighborhood life without timeframes, accountability, or guidance. I was moving and absorbing without a compass.

Our neighborhood was filled with meanderers like me. There was nothing to anchor a kid to his home, as most of us had several brothers or sisters competing for space in the mostly two-bedroom houses, and few radio programs geared to kids as listeners. To ease the household congestion, we kids were routinely told to "go outside and play," with no restrictions on bad weather; if there was snow or ice, we were told to simply just wrap up warm and get out there! The routine to hook up with a friend was to stand outside the front door or window of the kid's house and yell his name to come out, since there were no telephones in homes yet. Kids hung together in small groups, roaming the streets to find the day's challenge.

One favorite pastime was pulling a wagon to the top of a steep street, using one foot to push off to a fast start, and jumping into the wagon before it raced off without you, and then soaring downwards into the busy street, dodging cars.

"You're going to get yourself killed!" the adults frequently admonished us.

We ignored them.

We were accustomed to walking long distances to parks to play ball or downtown to see a movie or to the train tracks to hop a train for a joy ride, jumping off just before it picked up maximum speed. We knew the danger—we just knew it wouldn't happen to us. I got a two-wheeler bike when I was thirteen to run my paper route, which greatly increased the distance I could explore, but decreased my time to explore. I had to be up at five to deliver papers and pester the customers to pay their paper fee, which I had to collect.

After two years of delivering papers, I took a job pushing an ice cream cart. I learned from these menial jobs not to get stuck doing them for the rest of my life!

As time went on and I grew older, I had to find my own direction in this freefall environment. I drifted away from a roaming-the-neighborhood life but was moving and absorbing without a compass. I learned to pull myself out of life's ditches and began to wander and travel away from home, either by hopping on freight trains or hitchhiking, without giving my parents notice of my departure. I was on my own life search, driven by an innate, adventurous spirit that would never leave me.

I had heard a lot of reminiscent conversations about or references to the Mexican Revolution during my stay in Mexico, but the "War" everyone was talking about when I returned to the US was an unknown mystery to me. People would gather on the street corner in El Paso and listen together to a radio someone had turned on, to hear the latest news about bombings, air and sea battles, and countries where our troops were engaged in battle. They would slap each other's backs in encouraging gestures, or high-five a bystander, or curse vehemently any enemy destruction of our troops or territory. If the group of listeners was very excited or hushed and attentive, I would squeeze in to listen.

Since I was in the crowded downtown area a lot, I got the latest news daily. Once or twice a week I would go into a movie house—partly to see the show but mostly to see the black-and-white war news reels. I would sit back with the hamburger I sneaked in and have my lunch with my eyes glued to the screen, fascinated by the war ships and fighter planes. Ground battles with sound made me feel the action.

This, I began to understand, was World War II, into which America had been irreversibly pulled when the Japanese bombed Pearl Harbor, Hawaii, in 1941, the very year I had left for Mexico. At this time, 1943, television had not yet become a household fixture. Radio was the main news source and many people didn't even have that, as only 10 percent of homes had full electricity as of 1935; more had it now, but the country was nowhere near full service in all homes. Few families had telephones in their homes. The daily newspaper was another news source to which only a sparse number of the population subscribed, because many people didn't choose to read or did not know how to read, and so they waited for news from neighbors or any available radio.

The first bells of impending war, I learned, had tolled in 1939 as Hitler invaded Poland. Then, the American population was strongly isolationist and wanted no part of a war so far away. "Just keep it over there!" was a common refrain. President Franklin Roosevelt was keenly aware that the war would eventually come to our shores, given the conquering fanaticism of Hitler and his partner in world domination, Italy's Mussolini. Roosevelt created America's Lend Lease Act, authorizing sale, lease, transfer, or exchange of arms and supplies to any country that the US President deemed to be in vital need of military support in fighting the onslaught of the Axis powers. This allowed swift and ample dispersal of US weaponry such as tanks, ships, armaments, and planes to England and Russia, which were taking the brunt of invasion and bombing from the Axis powers: Germany and Italy. The third Axis power was Japan. Until December 1941 Japan had primarily focused on invading China, doing severe pillaging and raping in their invasions, but then they made their greatest military misstep and attacked the huge American fleet stationed in Hawaii. In "awakening a Sleeping Giant and filling him with a great resolve," they led President Roosevelt to declare war during a speech where he said that the bombing of Pearl Harbor on December 7, 1941, was "a day which shall live in infamy."

Once the newsreels were out and Americans saw the massacred sailors floating in the Pacific and the sinking of great American naval ships, explosive support for the war swept across the country. No longer was anyone an isolationist; instead, Americans were inflamed with a desire for justice and revenge. They shifted full throttle into attack mode. American men and women rushed to join all branches of the armed services, and American industrial growth surged forward to increase and catch up on equipment production. Within four years, America's war effort produced the most compelling and dominating world presence and thriving economy.

During this time, the song lyrics of "Over There"—written in 1917, during WWI—were heard again:

Over there, over there, send the word over there
That the Yanks are coming, the Yanks are coming
The drums rum-tumming everywhere.
So prepare, say a prayer,
Send the word, send the word to beware,

We'll be over, we're coming over,
And we won't come back till it's over
Over there!

My friends and I would sing along when we heard it. We were all in it!

At the dawn of World War II in 1941, the US population had last been counted as 132,000,000, 56.5% of which lived in urban towns or cities and 43.5% of which were in rural farm areas. Many of the armed forces were comprised of farm boys who had never been off the farm. During the war another song became famous, this time for the words, "How Ya Gonna Keep 'em Down on the Farm (After They've Seen Paree)?" After the war's end, many of them went to college on the GI Bill or settled in cities to escape returning to the humdrum of farm life.

The more newsreels I saw about the war, the more fascinated I became. I wanted to know about every battle and listened eagerly to the explanatory commentaries.

Neighbors would sit outside on their front porches in the evenings and talk about the war news daily. Sometimes I had new input they had not yet heard from the movie newsreels I frequented—or from my interaction with servicemen.

When servicemen came home on leave, people would besiege them for their personal war stories. They were especially responsive to young guys like me and my friends. We would tail them as we sighted them walking down the streets or sitting at a restaurant bar to eat, and if we got a chance to talk to them, we barraged them with questions about their war involvement. They didn't need any prompting; they seemed to really want to tell their stories, not at all sparing the gruesome or soul-wrenching experiences they'd had. It wasn't a brag session, though. A lot of remorse seeped into their tales about the death they had caused, whether purposely or inadvertently. More than a few said they missed their mom.

One day, I saw a soldier in uniform sitting on the ridge of the Alligator Pit, which held several alligators in the middle of the downtown park and was a big attraction to park visitors. I could tell he was Mexican, so as I passed by I spoke to him in Spanish.

"You stationed at Fort Bliss?" I asked in Spanish.

He answered in Spanglish: "Sí, at Fort Bliss." He looked kind of frail.

"You been sick?" I asked.

He seemed to want to unload his story. "Yes, I'm sick. I was much worse but am better now. I got malaria in Burma."

"I had diphtheria as a kid," I said. "Is it like that?"

"Well," he said softly, "it killed a lot of my comrades. You get it from mosquitoes, and the jungles of Burma are full of them. The jungles are scorching hot and rain-drenched all year, with mobs of mosquitoes that you can't get away from—not even by wearing lots of protective clothing or smearing repellants on you. They're just going to have you. We were there to build a road. I got sick early, so I didn't have to be there long, thank God, but I still nearly died of the fever. I went there to fight men, not insects. It's a hopeless battle. Some of my soldier friends died of it and were buried there in the jungles of Burma. We had to leave them because there was no way to get them through the jungle. There were no rescue Jeeps or airstrips for planes to land. We just dug shallow burial holes and left them there. There was really no way to mark the graves in the jungle." He sighed. "We thought we were next. I got the malaria at the end of trudging through the jungle to our targeted destination and was rescued by a small unit of medics that had enough meds to keep me alive until a larger Army unit could transport me to a temporary medical facility. That saved my life, and I was flown back here."

"Are you from here?" I asked.

He shook his head. "I was raised in Mexico and came here to El Paso to join the Army. I wanted to see the world and become a US citizen. I saw nothing but jungle."

"Well," I told my new friend, "I guess that's a real crush down."

"Yes," he said, "but I still want to be in the Army and go overseas if I can. I have nothing to go back to Mexico for. This is my only chance for a career. Maybe I can move up in the ranks and become an officer if I stay in long enough and stay alive. I pray for God's help."

It seemed to relieve him a bit to talk. He was a border kid—just like me, except from the other side. We felt a common connection to each other through our language and culture, and we were only separated by a few years—the years that had kept me out of this part of our country's history by being too young to participate. The movie reels showed loud, patriotic music, fighter plane battles, and massive gunships cross firing. What I saw in this boy was different. In him I saw a quiet agony—but agony with hope.

It was a side of the war not shown on the movie reels.

Patriotic fervor was high in the US. Soldiers stationed at Fort Bliss and Biggs Field in El Paso were accorded respectful glances or nods by the population as they filled the downtown streets on their brief leaves from duty. Mexican immigrants joined the US military with the hope that they could be eligible for citizenship after the war. Young men of age flocked to join the service, carried by the pervading gush of loyalty to the cause of American victory.

In the two years after my return, I learned a lot about the war from US soldiers and airmen stationed at the local bases, as they waited to be shipped out to fight and as they returned between duty assignments. None of them seemed to have relished their experiences, and they certainly didn't glamorize the war, but the wonder they held for all the foreign lands, ocean travel, and cultures into which they had been immersed really impressed me and ignited a fierce desire to roam and see the unknown as they had. The armed forces became an escape route I looked forward to availing myself of when I was of age. I was especially fascinated by the big ships, carriers, and destroyers that traversed the world's oceans and visited foreign countries I passionately wanted to see and know about.

I committed myself to one day becoming a sailor.

Almost everyone knew a person who was in the war effort or who had a son, dad, husband, brother, or other relative who was off at war. They all had tales of letters they'd received telling of the brutality they'd encountered and inflicted. A few times, the soldier's letter arrived after he had died. That was extreme pain the whole neighborhood heard of quickly, and when it did, it grieved with the family of loss. Wreaths were hung on the doors of the lost son, and families wore black to express their pain. The most prevalent feelings of the relatives of the soldiers at war were anxiety and constant wonder about their whereabouts and the constant danger to which they were exposed. Attendance at church services was high, as we all solicited God to protect our warriors, which included many women serving alongside the men. It was probably my age that slanted my interest to the adventure of the war stories and not the danger. Instead of becoming discouraged or cautious, my intrigue grew.

It eventually seemed the war was a perpetual fact of life in the US. Americans became accustomed to practicing for possible bombing raids over our skies by dousing any light after dark during the hours of practice. We would sit around the radio in the evening when school, work, and household activities like laundry and dinner were done and listen to music, news, or voice-acted stories. Even the limited light that shone from the face of a home radio had to be covered so no overhead plane could spot and use it as a target of a populated area. People knew that they could only light a match long enough to light one cigarette so that no light would last long enough for an overhead enemy pilot to pick it up as a target. Four years of perpetual war made us all feel as if it might last forever.

Then, the great miracle all Americans had solicited of God occurred: Germany surrendered unconditionally on May 7, 1945. Italy was already out of the war, as Benito Mussolini had been killed with his mistress as they tried to escape the wrath of the Italian population who'd had enough of the war. Mussolini's wife was hung upside down with her dress hanging open, exposing her underwear, after the mob murdered her. Japan, however, entrenched with the belief that suicide was preferable to surrender, steadfastly continued their hopeless fight.

Thousands of American soldiers were sure to die in an invasion of Japan, so President Truman, who had succeeded President Roosevelt upon his death, made the decision to expend no more American lives and gave the order to drop the atomic bomb.

The first atomic bomb, Little Boy, was dropped on Hiroshima, Japan on August 6, 1945, killing 80,000 Japanese civilians. Still, that did not persuade Emperor Hirohito to surrender. Three days later, on August 9, a second bomb, Fat Man, was dropped on Nagasaki, Japan, killing 40,000 more Japanese. This finally compelled the Emperor to surrender unconditionally.

The movie reels of the atomic bomb explosions made it seem like science fiction had invaded our world, and many wondered if such power and destruction would design the world's future. Would we one day become victims of our own country's warfare invention?

I was eleven years old and in downtown El Paso, Texas with my mom when suddenly the crowd was ignited with newspaper sellers yelling, "The War is over!" and "Extra, extra, read all about it!"

The day was September 2, 1945. People were screaming and hugging and forming snake lines weaving up and down the street. It was an all-day and all-night event, spontaneous and increasingly packed as the word-of-mouth news spread to more people. Japan had signed the Instrument of Surrender aboard the USS Missouri (BB-63). No more American soldiers returning in caskets! The US celebrated in bursts all over the country. America had bought, fought, and paid for the world's freedom.

I knew all the major battles that had been fought and the names of the top generals, like MacArthur, Patton, and Eisenhower. I knew the names of important carriers, destroyers, bombs, and more—like the Enola Gay, which had dropped the first atomic bomb in the history of the world. I would never forget the films of the war I had seen at movie houses, both of battles and of depleted and destroyed civilizations. I felt a surge of pride at being a member of the most powerful conquering country in the world.

Mexicans' talk of the Revolution's end had been full of uncertainty, confusion, and a sense of resignation. America's talk of the end of this War, in contrast, was blatantly and boisterously celebrated with relief and pride. We believed God had bestowed victory on us because ours was a righteous cause. Feeling ordained by almighty power, the entire citizenry surged forth to build on America's position and recognition as the greatest Power on Earth—one that would never be defeated and whose citizens would experience deserved prosperity through all times. The economy boomed. Spirits could not be dimmed. America was the all.

Part II: Patricia

CHAPTER 8

Another Kid's War Years

LIFE WAS SIMPLE AND quiet, burning hot in the humid summer and freezing in the snow and ice-pelted winters. On September 2, 1945, my world was Emerson Street in St. Louis, Missouri.

I was two months from my sixth birthday, in bed at the first show of night descending, swooning toward sleep. As nightfall encroached, I heard a loud yelling from a few people and what sounded like pots and pans being banged together.

"Patty! Larry!" my mom and dad yelled. "Come outside!"

My brother, Larry, stepped with me onto the front porch and headed down onto the grassy terrace—and saw, in amazement, what were initially a few adults and kids grow into a yelling, frantic crowd. Everyone was hugging each other and banging pans together to attract more neighbors; some were crying and screaming, "The War is over!"

"What's a war?" I asked my mom, clutching her skirt in my hand.

I don't remember getting an answer, but everyone was so excited I knew whatever it was, it was good that it was over. The whole neighborhood stayed excited for a long time. Strangers would smile at you as they passed on the street.

And then came my sixth birthday!

A birthday cake for me! How exciting.

I thought about it all day. I wasn't allowed to be in the kitchen when Mom made it so I wouldn't see it, which only made me more excited.

The family sat down to dinner that night and Mom or Dad announced that it was Patty's birthday. We ate as I anxiously awaited the meal's end, when my mom set the cake, candles lit, in the table's center and our family—my mom, dad, and brother—sang "Happy Birthday." Then I blew out the candles and was given one simple gift that I relished then but don't remember today. That was what a child's birthday was, mostly, in middle-class St. Louis in 1945. Kid's birthdays were simple then, and had not exploded into the major parties they are today.

I was six and my brother nine. World War II had ended. People were simple in their thinking, and middle-class wealth had not yet stamped itself on American culture.

Larry was my best friend and I greatly loved him—loved his kindness and mildness of manner, along with his adventurousness. He was always climbing things he shouldn't and racing up and down the alley with our neighbor David Frazier on a wagon, each boy taking turns shoving the other off on a ride and seeing how far they could go.

During the icy, frozen winters, we would make clay figures and set them on the outer frame outside the iced window and see how frozen they would get. We walked together to school—twelve long street blocks—with galoshes over our shoes to protect our feet from the ice. In pouring rain we sloshed to school and set our open umbrellas in the cloakroom to drip dry.

The nuns at school corrected swiftly, but not fearsomely, every possible infraction of correct behavior we could commit, and we of course confessed those infractions to the priest on Fridays.

Larry had asthma and often couldn't play outside, so we played cards: Follow Suit or Casino. Occasionally, our parents and some neighbors would play Pinochle at our kitchen table, with great vigor and laughter. Simple days!

The past summer, Larry and I had spent a couple of weeks on Grannie Anne's farm outside St. Louis. We entertained ourselves by pelting her two huge plow horses, Barney and Nellie, with corn cobs until they got incensed enough to chase us from their grazing area to the barn—a long distance.

Each time we ran, Larry made sure I kept up, and we climbed the barn ladder to the loft just before the horses arrived, raising their pawing hooves and snorting their anger.

One day, we realized we weren't going to make it to the barn.

"Pat, get into the wagon!" Larry yelled.

Just in front of us was a large wooden wagon filled with fresh corn cobs. Following Larry's lead, I jumped in and snuggled into the cob pile as the horses circled, frustrated.

We were afraid Grannie Anne would see what we'd done, but also kind of wished she would see our predicament and save us. Then Larry ventured to throw to one of the horses a fresh cob, and it sniffed it and began to eat. We threw out several more after that; the horses seemed to enjoy them, and they eventually wandered off.

Grannie Anne forbade us to go near her two vicious hogs, which weighed a few hundred pounds and did not like people. They were caged until slaughter time, and we wondered if they knew. We would run out to the hog pen, which was not within seeing range of our grandmother, climb the wooden rails that comprised the fencing around the hogs, and watch them snort at us and run threateningly up to the fence on which we precariously dangled for a close view.

One bored day, Larry decided to climb into the pen and ride the big hog. I screamed as loud as I could to alert Grannie Anne, "Grandma, Grandma! Larry's getting into the hog pen!"—but I knew she couldn't hear me.

Larry ran after the hog, jumped on it, and grabbed its ears, which panicked the hog. Larry hung on tight with his legs around the hog's ribs, yelling back at me, "I got him, I got him!"

As the hog slammed into the fence to derail him, I helplessly screamed, "Larry grab the fence! Get off. Get off!"

"I can't," he cried. "He'll kill me!"

I believed him. Grannie Anne always told us the pigs would kill and eat us if they could. I loved Larry so much, I ran in sheer panic toward the house, screaming for Grannie to come save him. She heard and met me halfway between her farmhouse and the barn, and we both raced hysterically toward the hog pen, screaming, "We're coming! Hold on!"

As we closed in right up to the ridge of the hog pen, Larry walked up to us layered with straw shreds, looking stunned but walking upright with a big grin.

"Did you see that, Pat?" he crowed. "I rode him!"

He acted all brave about it and told me he'd been doing fine and I had spoiled his fun by tattling. But he never went into the hog pen again and seemed to have lost his fascination with watching them after that day.

After our stay on the farm we went back to St. Louis and Catholic school, which led to my birthday dinner, in our small kitchen, in the cool fall of October.

Toward the end of dinner, Larry lifted a hidden gift from his lap and handed it to me. I was getting a second gift! From my brother!

"I found it in a section of the store counters where it looked different than all the other stuff," he confided as he put it in my hands. "I'm pretty sure it was in the wrong place; it's worth way more than what I paid for it."

I could see the expectation and excitement in his eyes as he sat across the table from me, holding my gaze. I slowly, and with amazement, unwrapped the paper.

On a card, a silver chain was draped, and from it hung a queenly, gorgeous, sparkling pendant—a necklace of such beauty as I had never seen! There were ten glass, circular gems, each encased in silver—four in the first row, three in the second, two in the third, and one singular one dropping from the bottom.

Someone put the necklace on my neck. Larry grinned widely, and so did I. I secreted and savored my only necklace, and when, a few years later, we moved and drove the three-day trip (in Dad's first car, with no air conditioning) from St. Louis to El Paso, Texas—a better climate for my brother's asthma—I took my Sorry game and my necklace.

I wore that necklace on endless dates as I maneuvered the years from my first date, at age fourteen, through to about twenty-one, before I laid it in my jewelry box and lifted out a different necklace—something more in keeping with the current fashion. I always got compliments on Larry's necklace.

Somehow the chain broke eventually, and I meant to fix it but didn't know where to take it. Then, after many years and a marriage, more moves, and kids, I suddenly couldn't find it again. It had been my secure link to my life and childhood years in St. Louis, like a key to my lost past and, for sure, a token of the great love my big brother and I had for one another. I was devastated by the loss. My heart would leap if I could have back my favorite necklace ever!

We had my sixth birthday dinner in the two-bedroom house with red brick siding my dad had bought and brought, with his carpentry skills and two years of labor, from a forlorn low-income-looking house to a nice refurbished home. By the time my father was done, we had an indoor bathroom, a kitchen with updated lighting and plumbing, a yard with a profusely green lawn, shrubbery, flowers, a vegetable garden bearing giant juicy tomatoes, a cement sidewalk in front and back, a garage, and an ash pit in which to burn fall leaves and trash, all tidily encompassed by a new white picket fence.

My father, Ed Akin, was always either gone to his job all day or working in the yard or basement or on the roof, recreating from scratch our new home. He was born on a Kentucky farm and was a master hunter and marksman, a pugilist, and ice skater. He'd learned his carpentry skills from his dad, whose ancestry originated in England's rural area and who was a descendant of brothers who immigrated in the late 1800s to the United States from England, where they had all worked in the English shipyards. My dad had eventually moved with one of his brothers from Kentucky to the crowded and bustling metropolitan city of St. Louis, which by the 1940s had grown to a population of over 816,000 and become a major railroad center in the US.

Most men then had skills like house, barn, and fence building and repairs that had been passed down by their fathers through the centuries, and which were essential in maintaining their farms or small city homes. The days of calling specialists like painters, electricians, plumbers, roofers, or window glass installers had not yet surfaced, and most men were expected to fix their own property with the possible help of a neighbor (to whom the favor would be returned at some point).

Nearly half of Americans during this time lived in rural areas on farms, raising crops or animals for their own use or in great enough amounts to sell. Some farming families sent their children to small country schools or taught them to read at home, if the parents themselves could read, but illiteracy was part of country culture. Most rural schools were not in session in the spring and summer months, as all family hands were needed for crop planting, reaping, cattle or pig slaughtering, and preserving for the winter's food supply. Vegetables had to be canned, which meant cleaning, cooking, and putting them into air-sealed bottles placed into an underground cellar to preserve as a winter food supply—thus the name of "preserves," which still identifies jams and jellies in modern-day markets.

Although I was born and raised in St. Louis, my mother's mother lived on a farm outside of the city (the farm where Larry and I visited her and lived the country life for a couple weeks each summer). Running through the fields of cornstalks, harvesting vegetables, snapping green beans, petting newborn calves, slopping the pigs, and playing in haystacks were daily routine before the modernization of animal and plant production and processing.

In the 1940s, farm life began at dawn: You had to feed and water the herds and collect the chicken eggs, which were a daily staple. Cows were milked daily by hand and the milk was brought into the kitchen to "process," which meant separating the milk from the cream or, sometimes, applying flavoring and ice to make ice cream. There were no freezers to save the ice cream, so it had to be eaten when made.

The egg-giving chickens also were used for meat: when this was the case, they were beheaded on a tree stump and let loose to run without their heads attached the short distance until they fell, then were put into boiling water to loosen the feathers, plucked, and then cooked into the family's dinner. Chickens were kept in a chicken pen in which they roamed freely. There were racks stuffed with straw in a shed where the chickens perched and slept at night and were kept safe whenever a blizzard hit. There was also a small shed, called the "jail," where my grandmother Anne placed a chicken if it was a "hen pecking" victim. This occurred fairly often: a hen, for no apparent reason, would single out one chicken to be pecked on the head. The attacking hen would soon be joined by a flock of chickens, which, over a few days' time, would murderously peck the chicken's head raw to the skull, until it died. To save it, my grandmother placed the chicken in the "jail" on a straw bed with food and water until it healed. Once its head was no longer raw and did not invite pecking, it could be safely released back into the farm's chicken population, which by then was over the pecking rage or had picked another chicken to "hen peck."

During one brief two-week summer stay on the farm, a chicken hatched a batch of chicks and I was allowed to keep one for my pet. It had soft yellow fur before its young feathers appeared, and it snuggled into my neck at night to sleep. I was in love with my baby chicken and named it Chicken Peter. I would leave it in a safe box during the day with food, as my cousin Carol and I went running through the cornstalks into the wind or climbed the ladder into the barn hayloft where the cut hay was thrown. We collected eggs and went to the pond out in the fields to watch the turtles or chase rabbits. We watched our Grannie Anne milk cows and make delicious creampuffs.

We also went with our grandpa and grandma to the country store, where Grannie Anne left produce to be sold to other farmers and bought produce to add to her groceries. She also bought chicken feed in what were called "feed sacks," which came in a variety of beautiful materials that women would buy, wash, and use as material to make clothes. Grannie Anne would pick a pattern and buy the same one on her monthly visits to the store until she had enough to make a dress with her tabletop sewing machine, as did many of the farm wives. They would be distraught if the pattern was discontinued before their dress was finished.

On our infrequent visits out to Grannie Anne's farm, which was miles outside the city of St. Louis, I would see and cuddle my Chicken Peter. The chick's growth was rapid and always a surprise, but I still always knew which chicken among the others was mine.

On one visit, my mom, dad, brother, and I arrived in time for Sunday dinner at Grannie Anne's farmhouse. I ran first to see my chicken before taking my seat at the table, but he wasn't there.

I ran back inside. "Where's my chicken?" I asked my grandma.

"I hadn't noticed it was missing," she said (rather suspiciously, I thought) as she set the freshly cooked chicken on the table to be carved.

My heart dropped. "Grandma, *where* is Chicken—"

"Patty," my mother said in a warning tone. "Don't ask about the chicken again."

My throat grew a lump. I knew the chicken on the platter must be Chicken Peter.

In those days kids did not question, argue with, or disobey their elders, so I just sat through the dinner without eating and didn't talk about it.

I held a grudge about Chicken Peter for a while, but with the swift path of life and my parents' talk about moving out of St. Louis to a place called Texas, which would be a healthier climate for Larry's asthma, I eventually mostly forgot my pet chicken. For a long time, though, I could still feel it on my neck if I closed my eyes.

Rural life was isolating; few neighbors were within walking distance, and there was little leisure time, as the daily work demanded to keep up the livestock and crops was laborious.

Water was still pumped from the outdoor and underground water reserve, with a three- or four-foot pipe installed over the water source, and a handle attached for an adult to grab and move forcefully in an upward and downward stroke that sucked the water up through the font and then spewed it into the waiting bucket sitting below. There were no quick drinks of water.

After dinner, with no streetlights to extend the day, the darkness came quickly. Candlelit lamps gave enough light for a farm wife to sew or knit while listening to the radio broadcast news, music, or a few half-hour shows with characters portrayed by voice actors, with no visuals like TV having yet been invented. Whole families would sit together in the short evenings listening to shows like *Amos and Andy* or *My Friend Irma* or similar family-geared shows. Each listener had their own image of the character's physical appearance, and when television did dawn a decade later, the same popular shows were presented visually on the screen to many of the same audiences and flopped because the characters did not appear as the audience had imagined them and they lost interest, as though their favorite character had died! There were no R-rated productions yet. Disinterested children were told to be quiet as adults listened to newscasts, which were their only exposure to national and, in extremely rare cases, international news.

American cities' availability of electricity and home telephone service, in contrast, had exploded. Returning soldiers marrying and finding employment boosted income, and the middle class swelled.

CHAPTER 9

From Roof Jumping to Chest Thumping

THE REVVING UP FOR World War II and the four years of our participation in the war had been a dynamic boost to the American economy. The production of war machinery yanked the country out of a depression that had started on Black Tuesday, October 29, 1929, but had its true beginning on October 24, the previous Thursday, on which day the stock market had collapsed and people who had lost great sums of money had actually jumped to their death from rooftops.

One immediate and visible effect of the dramatic downturn of expendable cash was the severely diminished presence of shoppers on Friday, November 29, 1929. The Friday after Thanksgiving had historically been the biggest shopping day in America, as eager customers did their early Christmas purchasing of gifts and decorations, but that year was a flop. Stores were severely crippled by lack of shoppers due to the recent financial collapse. The involvement of the

US in the war not only restored the American economy, but also made it the top world economy.

Trade, investment, and travel between countries expanded rapidly during this time, altering the political and financial power of all involved. As the US emerged as the greatest and most powerful survivor of the war years, it began a pattern of profuse aid to nations, even prior enemies who were in ruins or had been economically devastated by the War. Even in countries that had had a role in initiating the war, like Germany and Japan, the US established a democratic government and guaranteed military protection—actions that today are considered by many Americans to be an overextension and too vast an expenditure.

The war had changed the entire culture of the US. Women for the first time had entered the workforce in masses, breaking the employment ceiling. Many had become trained nurses in the armed forces or excelled in other work areas. Some remained in the military or civilian workforce even after the war ended. All military who returned to America's shores came with an extended experience with foreign lands, their cultures and languages, and many soldiers were even permanently stationed overseas in American bases that were established to protect the boundaries gained and reestablish civilizations that had been destroyed by the war. Foreign brides came to America on the arms of their American soldier husbands. Many immigrants who had served in the US military acquired the promised citizenship and became part of the American culture, infusing their own language and customs into the mix.

Isolationism had met its demise. The world had changed forever, and America was leading the change.

During the 1940s, American housewives were still using clotheslines with wooden clothespins to hang their newly washed laundry outside. Washing machines were big round tubs on legs that moms wheeled up to the kitchen sink and filled with water before inserting the dirty laundry with soap and plugging the machine into the electric wall outlet to make it swish back and forth for about fifteen minutes until the clothes were clean. That done, each item was lifted out individually and carefully inserted into the upper, non-electric part of the machine called the "wringer."

The wringer was two rolling pins fitted snugly together and turned by a side handle to squeeze out the water in which the clothes had been washed. The clothes were slowly pulled through the wringer, and then the next item was inserted. It was dangerous in that if the person inserting the clothes stuck their hand too far into the wringer rollers, their fingers would be pulled in between the wringers and mashed or even broken.

Clothes washing day, in short, was sloppy and laborious.

Thanks to the technology and machinery inventions of the war, all of this changed in the 1950s, and America was given "*Ozzie and Harriet*" moms. These mothers of American families could now buy automatic clothes washing machines they stuffed their laundry into and walked away from to let the clothes wash and wring dry without any attending.

This industrial revolution yielded other machinery that modernized all facets of American culture: refrigerators with the capacity to make ice cubes, and vacuum cleaners that released women from previously tedious labor. Televisions also slowly invaded most family living rooms. The programs came on at about noon, and provided family shows about

American family life in black and white, with simple family stories presented in weekly series that endorsed proper family conduct, illustrated with comedic situations that usually involved child misbehavior quickly solved by humorous parental skill. Families gathered around for evening television viewing and identified with the characters.

The greatest and earliest family hit of the 1950s was *Ozzie and Harriet*, played by actual members of a family (the Nelson family), and was popular for fourteen seasons. With over 435 episodes, *Ozzie and Harriet* engrained into the American culture the model family to emulate in dress, speech, and action.

Thus evolved the *Ozzie and Harriet* moms, which were American housewives who seemed to use these characters as their standard of conduct and who saw these TV families as perfect stereotypes to emulate. Another family comedy series of the '50s was *Leave it to Beaver*, which portrayed a mischievous little boy, Beaver, consistently getting into simple neighborhood mischief that was compassionately and swiftly resolved by his dad, who was always punctually home for dinner to supervise family behavior. The mother, June, performed her cooking and house cleaning in a "Sunday go to Meeting" dress and pearls, her hair impeccably styled. She also was never stressed or out of sorts.

These shows, which engulfed the country, were an absurd and lofty image to try to achieve or live up to, as no one's kids were so easily manipulated or controlled, and few dads were always home on time and eager to indulge in family therapy. So, not all *Ozzie and Harriet* moms were happy. Yes, they wore dresses, as shorts and pants were not yet accepted daily dress for women, but the dresses for daily house wear were actually referred to as "house dresses" and were older dresses no longer fit to go out in. Most women felt a bit shorted in their ability to match the TV mothers' perfection but continued to watch, perhaps hoping their children would behave and respond more like Beaver, and their husband would learn to deport himself more like the TV dad.

What were real '50s moms like? They were mostly housebound mothers with somewhere between three and six kids. Their entire existence was centered on raising their children and accommodating their husbands. With the advent of more freedom of time (due to the household machinery now available), many had small neighborhood group get-togethers with other stay-at-home moms, usually weekly or monthly "coffees," which allowed one lady to provide a nicely set table of coffee cups, saucers, and a canister of hot coffee. Another lady would contribute by baking a cake, and thus the ladies would enjoy their only solo social time.

In the '50s, women were just barely learning to drive a car. Families having a car was a new event in the typical middle-class neighborhood. Jokes about "women drivers" were as abundant as "dumb blonde" jokes, and were enjoyed by women as much as by men.

This inescapable and simplistic *Ozzie and Harriet* mom culture was only circumvented by the 1960s advent of birth control pills, which gave women greater control over childbearing and to which most women responded quickly by limiting their family size. With their formerly totally encompassing family duties lightened, women also became interested in a college education, which until then had always, by lack of access, eluded them. They started the march toward higher education, which gave them an opening to occupy professional positions in the workforce and thus allowed them to become participants in the money game. Equality was raising its head and replacing women's house dresses with office suits.

Today, America has graduated from carports that sheltered one family car to two- and even three-car garages. Freeways engulf the nation. The fallout explosion of World War II is still in action.

And the *Ozzie and Harriet* moms? They're now *The Devil Wears Prada* moms.

Part III: David

CHAPTER 10

Racing to Adulthood—Grabbing the Reins

IN EL PASO, MY dad had steadily maintained his fruit business during the war years and I had remained close to him in Juárez and El Paso, helping him. His fruit and vegetable supply intake from Mexico expanded. Customer demand for produce from US Southwest states, Juarez, and El Paso grew fast. I was pressed into the fruit business. He opened at sunrise every morning, taking me along if I wasn't in school. I was busy, but I was also restless.

I had grown back into my original culture and language and entered my early teen years. Although I now had a bigger hand in my dad's business, going on trips with him to collect or distribute his produce in Juárez and El Paso, I was also out of the house now most of the time, establishing my life with a network of friends and mischievous enterprises.

I always had a job: Besides working with my dad, I had my own ice cream cart to make money from. I also had a paper delivery route on which my close companion, my dog, Spotty, accompanied me daily. She was with me through all my childhood years, and as I left home for work or travel she was always at my dad's home, waiting for me.

I moved haphazardly into my teen years, greeting each day with routine activities without any specific goal in mind. I rode my motorcycle, which was the activity I enjoyed most, and which allowed me to leave town with other friends who had their own bikes. We rode to Ruidoso, New Mexico; Las Cruces, New Mexico; and all points between and further, racing through rough terrain and breaking highway speed limits, stacking up traffic tickets but loving the life of freedom and adventure. We met drifters, serious cycle gangs, and just a lot of interesting characters—some to avoid, and some to connect with, hear their stories, and move on. Boredom never entered into our missions of exploration.

During summer vacation, a friend of mine, Clark Benson, said he wanted to go visit his mom in California. His parents were divorced and he was living with his father in El Paso, and he missed his mom. Since we were only fifteen years old in 1950, we made up a story for our parents that we were going to a Boy Scout camp in Ruidoso, New Mexico. My dad gave me forty dollars to go, but Clark's dad only gave him ten dollars.

The railroad yard was only one street behind my house, so we went there and asked a railroad worker when a train to Oxnard, California would be leaving. He said there would be a long drag hauling empty cars leaving in three hours, so we hurried home and packed some small bags of clothes. I put my money into the inside pocket of my boot for safekeeping.

Back at the yard, we sneaked around the train workers and found a moving open car out of view, and some hobos reached their hands out to help pull us in as the train picked up speed. We moved to the back of the car and had our first good look at our traveling companions: six raunchy, smelly people who were already sprawled out for the ride and consuming most of the car space. They looked steely-eyed and unfriendly, but we figured they knew how to do train hopping. We noticed that they all had water bottles, too, and we knew immediately we were in trouble: we hadn't even thought about water, and the freight car was hot and stuffy due to its steel construction, probably about 100 degrees.

They were all gringos, Anglos, shabbily dressed and filthy. The oldest, toothless one in the group said, "If you want to share our water, it will cost you a dollar."

We agreed, unquestioningly, because they were scary-looking guys.

As we rounded the railroad bridge leaving El Paso, Mt. Christo Rey disappeared in the distance and new vistas opened up. We were excited that we had left on our trip but were also feeling nervous about sharing a car with these threatening-looking guys.

We had traveled about five hours when our train stopped to allow another one that was traveling east to pass. It was very dark in the car—it was about 10:00 p.m.—and I was dozing uneasily when I felt someone suddenly straddle my body.

I opened my eyes. The old, muscular, intimidating-looking man of the group was sitting on me and holding an ice pick, or maybe a long-bladed knife, to my skin right under my chin. My friend simultaneously jolted to a sitting position, frozen, as I was, in fear.

"Empty your pockets and give me all your money!" the man ordered me.

I pulled my Levi's pockets entirely inside out so he could see I had nothing but a pocket knife.

"Take off your boots," the man growled. I did, and he took them and ran his hands down into them. Luckily, he missed the secret pocket holding my money.

"The only one of us who has money is my friend here," I said. "He has about ten dollars. He's holding our money."

The man angrily threw my boots back at me and moved toward Clark, who eagerly, but sheepishly, dug out his ten dollars and showed the man his otherwise empty pockets, hoping to be spared any assault. The guy snatched the money wordlessly, returned to his side of the car, and went right back to sleep. We stayed awake the rest of the night.

After what felt like countless torturous hours, we pulled into Indio, California, and Clark and I made a rapid jump off the train as soon as it slowed enough that we thought we'd survive the landing, hoping no one would follow us. We breathed sighs of relief when no one did.

As the train pulled forward into the station, we spotted the Greyhound Bus Depot. We ran across the street to get there, watching the train slow for another two minutes before it came to a leisurely stop. I went to the pay phone, called the police, and told them that we had witnessed a bludgeoning of a hobo on the train, giving them the number of the box car and tediously describing the hobos we'd ridden with. "We were on the train too," I told them, "but we escaped after the beating. They threw the man from the train about twenty miles east of the Indio train stop . . . he might have been dead, I don't know."

I went on to say that the hobos had held knives to our throats and threatened our lives, and had talked in low voices amongst themselves about plans to pitch us from the train, as they said they had done to other train riders, after slicing us up. So we jumped while the train was still moving.

About three minutes after my call, five patrol cars surrounded the box car we'd described and, after kicking and knocking them down, placed the hobos under arrest and shoved them into the patrol car. We didn't feel guilty; we were sure these hobos had actually killed victims in exactly the way they'd threatened to harm us, and that they'd come very close to killing us the previous night.

We watched the whole thing go down from a secure place where we could not be seen, about two blocks away from the station. When it was over, we sat down at the restaurant in the bus depot, ordered ham and eggs, and had such a laugh of relief of tension and fear that we couldn't stop and could hardly eat. What a just payback! Our trip was off to a good start!

From now on we would know to be really careful about what kind of people we ended up around, and would hopefully have the adventure we'd planned.

After breakfast, we took sixteen dollars out of my secret boot pocket and bought two one-way tickets to Oxnard. We washed thoroughly in the bathroom, and boarded our bus with our bags of clothes, feeling clean and in high spirits.

Clark's mom had no idea we were coming. When he called, she came to pick us up from the bus depot, but she acted very put-upon. She was happy to see Clark but told me immediately, "You can spend the night, but tomorrow you have to get up early and leave."

Clark said nothing to help me stay at his mom's house, so I asked him if he was going to keep the promise we'd made to each other before we left—that we would stay together throughout the trip and our return to El Paso. He didn't say a word in response, which made it clear he had wanted my money and presence for the trip but had planned all along to cut me off as soon as we got there.

"I'll call your mom to send you money to get home," Clark's mom said. "But you have to leave tomorrow, whether I get hold of your mom or not. If I don't reach her, I'm calling the police tomorrow morning to come pick you up."

I would be on the street the next day. Clark's betrayal showed a complete personality change from the friend I thought I'd known. I asked him if he was hitchhiking home with me since my mom didn't even have a phone, and he didn't even answer me. He had planned to ditch me from the beginning.

After a short meal, and with repeated instructions from his mom to leave the next day, I fell asleep that night in the same room with my former best friend of two years, feeling afraid, desolate, very unwelcome, and unbelievably betrayed. He had become cold, unapproachable, silent, and distant the minute his mom first appeared.

I fell asleep immediately due to exhaustion, but awoke at daybreak in a panic, desperate to get away from the hostile environment. I grabbed my small pack and disappeared before anyone woke so I would not be taken away by the police. I walked back to Highway 101, about two blocks away—and saw water.

When I saw the beautiful, inviting Pacific Ocean rolling onto the hot beach, I decided to have a dip in the water. I pulled out my swimsuit and waded in. The water, which was slightly cold, woke me up and felt incredibly soothing for about half an hour. When I was done swimming, I went to the portable shower by the beach, showered, dried off with my old T-shirt, put on my only extra clean shirt and Levi's, and got onto the highway, hungry, with $1.50 in my pocket.

After holding my thumb out for just fifteen minutes, I got a thirty-mile ride to Los Angeles from a young college student. I told him how I'd gotten thrown out of my friend's house after spending all my money on the two of us. The guy drove me onto Hollywood Boulevard, gave me forty cents, saying that's all he had, and told me to go into the Roosevelt Hotel and go to the cook and he would give me a sandwich for the forty cents.

I walked into the hotel restaurant area, and the restaurant manager asked what I wanted. I told him, "I'm really hungry and I want to buy a sandwich." He told me to get out, so I found a fast food stand on a corner that was selling French dip sandwiches for fifty cents. I gulped one down. It was so good, and I was so starved, that I ordered another one.

Now I had only ninety cents in my pocket, but I wasn't worried; I felt like I was having the adventure I'd wanted! I hitched a ride on Hollywood Boulevard, and it took me about three or four rides to get out of LA. Each person gave me a little more change after I told them my story. By the fourth ride, I'd collected about another dollar.

My last ride was a guy in pickup truck with five teenage girls in the back. He dropped me off outside Bakersfield at dusk on a farm road. He told me in Spanish to go about a mile to the highway to hitch another ride, but by then it was pitch dark and I couldn't see a light or car anywhere. I walked blindly for about twenty minutes, and was suddenly very scared. I could not see anywhere. I couldn't even see to get off the road. I sat down on my bag and had a hard cry, then fell asleep with my head on my arms and my knees tucked close to my chest.

CHAPTER 11

Salvation or Annihilation

THE HONKING OF A car horn woke me up. All I could see were two headlights, and then a man stepped from the car and yelled, "Do you need a ride? Are you okay?"

I was so glad to see a person. "How far are you going?" I asked.

"Yuma, Arizona," he said.

I got into the car and shut the door. As we took off, I saw a boy who seemed about seven or eight years old asleep in the backseat. The man told me the boy was his nephew.

After three hours, during which I slept, the man woke me up.

"We're in Yuma," he said. "Let's go have some donuts and coffee."

I was so tired. "Can I stay in the car and wait with him?" I asked, pointing to the boy, who was still sleeping.

"Sure," the man said. "And I'm actually going on to San Antonio, so I can take you to El Paso on the way."

I'd never felt such relief in my life. I was finally okay and on my way home. No more dark roads or hunger.

The man returned from his donut snack and started driving again. About halfway out of Yuma, he stopped the car, pulled out a box of fried chicken, and offered me some. I greedily ate a few pieces—I had a young man's ravenous appetite—and they were incredibly delicious.

"Aren't you going to give your nephew some food?" I asked.

"No," he said, "he'll sleep all the way through."

I felt extremely uneasy about the condition of the boy, because he had by this point been asleep from midnight till noon, twelve hours. I had seen him move—only slightly and rarely, but I at least knew he was alive. The longer he slept, the more alarmed feelings began to arise in me.

The man, who was somewhere in his mid-thirties, very polite, well dressed in a sport shirt and slacks, and very well groomed, asked me if I could drive a couple hours so he could sleep.

"Sure," I said, glad to help him out. I took the wheel and started driving as he slept in a passenger seat. By this time, about 2:00 p.m., I was really suspicious that something was wrong with the kid in the backseat, who had now been asleep fourteen hours, so I trained the rearview mirror on him to watch him. He kept on sleeping for the next two hours of my drive, by the end of which I was convinced something sinister was going on.

When he woke up, the man reached in the back and brought out some sandwiches and Cokes. He took over driving, and we ate again.

About an hour later, as we were driving through a mountainous, rocky area called the Texas Canyon, the man pulled off to the side of the road.

"What are you doing?" I asked.

"I need to take a leak," he said, "c'mon with me."

I got out and also took a leak, facing away from him, to ensure my privacy and so not to be looking at him.

"Show me your dick," he suddenly said. "I want to see how big it is."

This surged spontaneous panic within me, and a desperate need to defend myself against him. "No, you got to be joking," I said, as I closed my pants fast.

"Let's sit down on the rock and have a Coke," he said. "I want to show you something." He went to his car for the Cokes. I watched him in the reflection of the windows when he opened the bottles, and as I watched, it appeared that he put something into one of the Cokes.

I looked around desperately for a quick way out of the desolate area, and found none. I was sitting with my hand resting on a fist-size stone, however, so I stuck it quickly into my boot. The man walked over to me and handed me the Coke; I took it and set it on the rock on which I sat as he sat down very close to me.

He pulled out some pictures that he had in his wallet and handed me one. It showed him sucking another men's penis. Another picture showed him with another man's penis stuck into his rear end as he sucked the penis of a third man.

I purposely hit the Coke so it spilled on the ground, my heart pounding frantically. This man was crazy, and he clearly planned to do something horrific to me.

"Do you want to do this with me?" he asked, pointing to the pictures.

"Mister, all I want to do is go home. Please take me home. Don't do this to me."

He looked at me as if he were sizing up my vulnerability. I believe he'd caught a glimpse of me stashing the rock in my boot, which had previously seen lying next to me and was gone upon his return from the car. I was also about an inch taller than he was, and I had a muscular build. I looked him straight in the eye as I spoke, disguising my terror, showing an aggressive readiness to defend myself, trying to communicate that I was not an easy target. I had mapped out in my mind exactly what to do to overcome him, and I think he saw that in my eyes and the alertness of my body. He had to know he might not win if it came to a struggle, given that he was of moderate stature and not the rough type. I'd gone through the flight-or-fight state when I first sought a way to run out, but I'd failed to find one, and I also felt tied to the kid in the car; I couldn't leave him. So I was a cornered animal, and my nature turned to fight mode: I collected and presented all the viciousness I could to deter him, though I was really afraid for myself and the little boy sleeping in the back, who I now knew was drugged.

"I won't do this to you," the man said in a very gentle, resigned voice. "C'mon, get back into the car and I'll take you to El Paso."

With a racing heart, ready to grab my rock for defense, I stiffly got into the passenger side, planning to bolt from the moving car if he touched me. He drove off as my mind raced, trying to grab on to a plan to get myself and the little boy out of this situation. I was so loaded with fear that time flew by without a word of conversation between us as I sat frozen.

In no time, it seemed, we passed the sign for the Las Cruces, New Mexico, city limits. I was vastly relieved to see it; it meant we were only thirty minutes from El Paso.

Finally, we got into El Paso.

"Which street do I take to get you home?" the man asked.

"Take a left on Mesa Street and another left on Montana

Street," I said, taking him to Lamar School, which was two blocks from my house. I didn't want him to know where I lived.

When he pulled over in front of the school, I leapt out of the car with a huge sense of relief. I took the rock out of my boot and threw it at the kid's window to see if he would move, and he did not. I had gotten the late-model Chevrolet car's color and CA license plate number, and I ran straight home to tell my mother to call the police.

I told my mom my story very fast so she would act before the guy got a good start to San Antonio. She was completely caught off guard; she still thought I'd been at Boy Scout camp. But despite her shock at my outpouring, she made the call.

After she hung up with the police, she began a drill of questions, trying to get filled in and understand what happened. I slowly told her the whole story. I'll never forget the amazed, wide, worried eyes of my mother as I gave her every detail.

I didn't know anything about pedophiles or sexual perverts then, as those things weren't a common topic of discussion in the schools or neighborhoods in the year 1949. TV had not made its debut, so other than vague general slurs regarding such acts, I had never seen or been versed on the facts. Because of that, I was not only instinctively frightened and repulsed by the advance, I was blurry on what was really going on, except that it was revolting, dangerous, and terrifying. In a matter of seconds, the soft-spoken, friendly man who had been so helpful to me had changed into an unknown, different being.

I now had a hyper-awareness of predators and how well they can disguise themselves. Over the years, I've maintained a real disgust regarding the assault attempted on me.

The police never came to the house to take a report. Maybe they acted on the call, or put out a bulletin. We never heard a response from them, so I'll never know what happened to the kid. Now that I have kids of my own, I sometimes see him asleep in the car and wonder, painfully, what happened, or how I could have saved him.

I never saw Clark again and never wanted to.

CHAPTER 12

A Batman Day

IT WAS BACK TO El Paso High. It was okay, I guess. I had friends and football there. But I really wasn't suited, I felt, to the humdrum and sedentary nature of learning—sitting in a chair with a desktop for forty-five minutes, and then, when the bell rang, moving to another chair with a desktop for another forty-five minutes, until, after six such rotations, interrupted only by lunch, I was free to leave and could resume the constant physical activity I craved.

Outside of school, I climbed mountains and explored caves, rode my motorcycle, and worked at whatever job I had at the time to make spending money, and I ran with friends who did the same. It was hard for me to sit still, and I felt captive in a boring setting at school.

I had always been strong and had a big build. There was a guy at school, a senior, who was stronger, however, and who excelled at showing off his big muscles and practicing fist blows on select victims. His body-building obsession included heavy weight lifting, and he was exceptionally proud of his massive biceps, which he displayed even in frigid weather by wearing scant T-shirts so all the students passing him in the hallways could not avoid noticing them. He would at random pick a guy in a lower grade to harass by walking up behind him, catching him off guard, and slamming his doubled, powerful fist into the victim's arm or shoulder. He'd laugh as the guy gasped and grabbed the injured area, then stroll off, victorious, through the throng of hallway students. Everyone stepped aside when he approached, so he considered himself untouchable royalty.

One week, this guy decided to hone in on me as his target. He took me by surprise and dealt the vicious blow to my right upper arm as he passed me in the hall one day. I guess it was fun for him so he did it again a few days later and, as was typical, walked off fast, laughing and making eye contact with the students who were his audience, as if he had achieved a physical feat and he expected an accolade.

I knew this guy outpowered and outsized me, but I planned to outmaneuver him to set him straight. I knew where he parked his car every day—always in the same place, by a brick building on campus—because on the days I borrowed my dad's car, I parked in the same area. I decided to catch him there by surprise.

After school the next day, as he opened his car door, I sprang out from behind the corner of the building with the baseball bat I had brought as his "lesson learner." I slammed one hard blow on his leg right beneath his knee, and he crumpled to the ground, screaming and crying in pain. He crawled frantically beneath his car and hid. I said nothing; I figured he understood the message.

He didn't choose me as his victim again.

Teen years of careless and increasingly aggressive motorcycle riding yielded massive traffic tickets that remained unpaid and eventually increased to an insurmountable debt to the city of El Paso. Patrol cops coordinated to get all the nonchalant bikers, into which category I must have fit, off the streets. During football season, while I was on the field practicing the game I loved, a detective arrived with a warrant for my arrest. I was taken to jail to wait for my appearance before a judge and pay the balance due—money I didn't have.

I was released on bond to await the court date. I stared at the ceiling at night, waiting for the date, knowing I could be given jail time if I was not able to pay the fees. My mind returned to a vision of an exploration I had often lapsed into, fantasizing myself on a great ship, with the ocean roaring in my ears and violent, wet winds engulfing my body as I adventured across the great Pacific Ocean—the turf of the great US Navy.

In a rush of enthusiasm and excitement, I acquired a fake birth certificate to establish my age as eighteen instead of my present and encumbering sixteen years, took it to the naval recruitment center, applied, and was accepted before even telling my parents of my new escape plan. My parents were struck with anxious foreboding for my safety, and talked to me about fixing my life and continuing in high school, but I was not persuadable. They knew me to be strong of opinion and, I think, even held a surge of hope that this may be a path of growth and solution for their son's demons of discontent, so they gave up the argument. I left for boot camp.

San Diego engulfed me. I felt lost in the space and rigid control of the chief petty officers, who supplied strict discipline, vigorous training, and inescapable regimen from 5:00 a.m. until 10:00 p.m. The only escape was the complete end-of-day exhaustion that hastened me into deep sleep on my narrow bunk-bed mattress. Shore leave was sparse.

Still, I was glad I'd joined up. I liked the feeling of being in a routine and group, and that sense of belonging kept growing.

After five months of my tour, my mother went through the legal maneuvers to correct my age on my enlistment and force me out of the Navy. I was back to my old, uneventful life, back in football and school, now with even further diminished interest. I was ready again for any escape.

CHAPTER 13

LA, Gypsies, Heists, Slim Living

I WAS GOING TO Ysleta High School when Art Perez got me out of my speech class by calling the school office and telling the clerk I was his brother and there was an emergency in my family. I went to the principal's desk and Art told me he had a guy who wanted us to drive his car to Los Angeles for fifty dollars. Only two months had passed since I had been pulled out of the navy by my mom and forced to go back to school.

"What are we doing in this fucked up town?" Art said. "My brother, Hank, is in LA and we can stay with him."

The same surge inside that had pulled me into the navy took over; I was already sick of school again. I put my books into my locker, and in two minutes I was jumping on the back of my motorcycle, which I had loaned to Art that morning, and we were ditching our ordinary, boring life.

We picked up the new 1952 Buick and the guy informed us that we had to take his deaf and mute, middle-aged brother to LA with us and drop him at a relative's house.

He also told us not to go over 60 mph, but as soon as we got onto the highway, we hit 90 mph just to see what the car could do, and then proceeded to stay mostly at that speed for the rest of the trip.

Driving that fast, we had a thrill, scared the poor brother pale, and got there faster.

After dropping the brother and the car in LA, we took our fifty dollars and caught a bus in downtown LA to see Hank, who worked at a laundry owned by his dad and uncle on Whittier Boulevard in East LA, a low-income, mostly Chicano area. Next to the laundromat was a restaurant called The Blue Cross. Hank said to wait there until he got off work and that a couple other old El Paso friends, Charles Bannon and Roy Stretz, were going to meet us. Bannon was sitting there alone when we walked in so we went over to see our good old friend, who had gotten to LA three weeks earlier with Hank and was out-of-the-ordinary happy to see us since he was broke and without a job. He was nursing a glass of water when we walked in, and he said he hadn't eaten in twenty-four hours, so we ordered six hamburgers with fries for a dollar and each ate two. We joked as Bannon told about his hapless adventures since he arrived, sleeping in Hank's car and trying to find work. He seemed relieved and hopeful now that we were there.

At about 6:00 p.m., in walked a group of Gypsies dressed in dirty, raggedy suits, speaking in a language I hadn't heard before. They seated themselves at a table near the jukebox, and put in ten cents for three songs, one being "Woolly Bully," and then one of them started tapping spoons together to the rhythm of the song and another one—he looked to be about seventeen years old—got up and started tap dancing and also playing spoons as he danced. It was the happiest, most fun-looking dance I'd ever seen.

We clapped him on wildly, laughing and yelling approval as he became more heated and really put on a show. When he finished, he sauntered around to all the customers to get money for his delightful exhibition. He got about a dollar in change and when he got to us we asked him to teach us to play the spoons. We exchanged names—his, he said, was Bingo—and then his friends, some of whom were young like him and some of whom seemed as old as forty, came over and filled up our table.

When we told our new friends we'd just arrived in LA and had no place to stay (Hank's uncle would not take us in, as Art had presumed he would), they said, "Just go across the street to that apartment house there and you can stay there for five dollars a week."

Art and I were so relieved; we immediately went to grab a room. The house was similar to my own family's place in El Paso, so I felt at home. The old Anglo woman warned us that she'd put us out if we let anyone else in, though, so we had to sneak Bannon in late at night to sleep on the floor. Stretz had a family to put him up.

Art and I got up very early the next day to look for a job. For hours, we walked around the industrial area, asking to be hired, but we couldn't find a job anywhere that Friday. The next day, Saturday, we saw all we could take in of East LA in one day by walking and riding buses, and then met up with the Gypsies at the same café that night. They did the spoon playing and dancing again, putting their hat in the middle of the floor for donations.

Bingo asked if we had money and we said no, knowing that he'd probably buy us something with the coins he had coming in—and he did. The oldest Gypsy even poured whiskey into the Cokes Bingo bought us. This was already more fun than school, and now that we had friends and a place to stay, we totally forgot the school thing. The Gypsies said we should go to work with them on Monday and they'd teach us how to make money.

On Monday, we jumped into the Gypsies' black, gangster-looking, 1937-model car with three of them and cruised the neighborhoods looking for dents in cars. When we found one, the oldest Gypsy went to the door in front of which the car was parked and we listened to him pitch her to let him fix the dent. He promised that for five dollars they would make it look like new. He was so honest and sincere sounding that she gratefully agreed and unlocked her car. We helped beat the dent outwards with a hammer as the other Gypsy mixed some clay with plastic to smooth out the remaining cleavage. Art and I spread the mixture out over the dent with our hands and watched, amazed, as the other Gypsies stole everything in the car (swiftly and without the car's owner detecting anything), got paid the five dollars, and left to find another victim. We did several cars that day and earned about thirty dollars legit, plus another seventy dollars in the sale of the stolen goods.

Art and I had honestly looked for a job and failed. So we just enjoyed our six-dollar cut, figuring we'd been left with no choice. We'd started out thinking we were going to learn a real trade, but we got over the shady side quickly because it was so much fun and kept us in hamburgers. After a week, though, we decided we were bound to get caught, so we quit.

When Friday came, the Gypsies took their only shower of the week and put on new twenty-five-dollar suits to replace the suits they had worked and slept in all week. It was their culture to change and wash weekly. Then most of the group went off to party, but Bingo decided to stay at the apartment, so we went back to The Blue Cross to meet Hank. Eventually, Bingo showed up and danced for our dinner, and at about 10:00 p.m., the rest of the Gypsies came in, mostly drunk.

The oldest Gypsy came right over to me and said that in his absence, a guy had moved into his apartment with his wife and three kids, and he wanted Art, Hank, Bingo, and me to go with him to beat up the intruder—in return for which he would give his car to me, Art, and Hank. We really needed transportation, so we talked it over and decided to help him and therefore help ourselves.

After finishing a bottle of whiskey, we drove to the Gypsie's place in the dark. When we arrived, we kicked down the door and stormed in to find a woman sitting on the toilet with the bathroom door open. There was no man in sight. The three kids were seated at the table waiting for their dinner, which was cooking on the stove, and they screamed in shock and fear at the angry shouts of their father, who began to slap and kick the mother.

At this, we all became frantic. The man was attacking his family. We had planned to run a man out of the premises, not be entangled in a family quarrel. The guy chased his wife out of the house as she screamed, "Police, please call the police!" She had cleared the house so we did too.

We all got into the slow-running car, full of a furious anxiety to get out of there, with Hank driving, and me hanging on to the running board, but the old Gypsy who had hired us saw us trying to get away and started chasing us. The car was so slow that he caught up and actually grabbed on to the bumper. We dragged him for about half a block (which was not too harmful to him, as the car moved at a snail's pace) before we stopped and he got into the car.

We went back to The Blue Cross and sat down to eat with a bottle of whiskey. The adrenaline had hit us by this point, and we thought the whole experience was fantastically funny and exciting, so we were having a fabulous, free-spirited celebration, until the old Gypsy told us the bottom line: we hadn't actually beaten up the guy, so we didn't get the car.

We quarreled with him over the justice of that, since we had kicked in the door and he'd run out and most likely gotten arrested, but the old Gypsy was firm.

During our negotiations to get the car, two sexy Anglo girls about our age walked in and started partying with us as Bingo put on his best show ever. The restaurant was full of cheering, clapping, stomping, screaming customers, all throwing money at Bingo. He picked up a lot of money and said, "Tomorrow I'm buying all our fares for a ride on the boat to Catalina Island."

We were ready to leave then—which worked out, because it was about 1:00 a.m. and the café was closing. We headed back across the street and went to sleep in high anticipation of the next day's fun.

The next day, Bingo kept his word: while all the other Gypsies went to the racetrack, he took Art, Hank, me, and the girls on the cruise to Catalina, where we spent the day swimming and drinking and dancing at a club. As the day wound to an end, we regretted having to get onto the last return boat to Long Beach.

After dropping off the girls, we met up with the rest of the Gypsies and partied on at The Blue Cross. The old Gypsy began agitating again for us to make a hit on his apartment the next day—try to find the right guy and beat him up and throw him out—but we talked him into letting us sleep on it, hoping we could get him to drop the idea and leave.

The next morning, we were awakened by five or six people's footsteps pounding up the stairs to our apartment, passing our apartment, and breaking down a door. They started beating up the entire Gypsy group we had been running with, including Bingo. We locked our door with the safety lock and watched through the transom window above our door as all their furniture was broken and thrown out of their second-story window—along with the old Gypsy. Soon, sirens alerted us that the police were near, and we heard the attackers running down the stairs to escape. The police caught them coming down and put them into a cop car.

The old Gypsy survived the fall but had to be taken to a hospital.

Bingo was badly beaten, with a busted nose and black eyes, so we took him to an emergency room, where we waited for his patch-up, and then took him to "The Office"—The Blue Cross. Bingo, as if nothing had ever happened, put money into the jukebox and started dancing wildly to "Woolly Bully," and the party was on again.

Despite the high-spirited camaraderie, I quietly decided myself then and there that I was through and getting out of this group before I ended up in a cop car.

I found a job two days later unloading train box cars of tile for $1.75 an hour, which was the most money I had ever made for work. It was eight to ten hours of hard labor per day; at night I was too tired to do anything—almost too tired to eat.

After a few days of this, I got off work to find Bingo waiting for me. He badly wanted to go see the condition of the old Gypsy, and asked me earnestly to go with him.

We found the old guy in a hospital bed with a broken collarbone, leg, jaw, and nose. He still mumbled that he would pay us money to go back to find the guy in his apartment and beat him severely, but it was all over; Bingo and I told him no, flat out.

It was time to go home and resume my life. I was still thinking about the pull of the navy—of living life on the ocean and seeing distant shores—but I was still too young.

Back in El Paso, my life was as uneventful as it had been when I'd left. I was so discontented that after a few months my dad signed for me to rejoin the navy, although

I was still only seventeen. I didn't have to go through boot camp again and was assigned on board a destroyer.

I was glad to be legally in the US Navy. I remembered the times I had opted out of my life in El Paso—jaunting off on sporadic adventures with friends, and getting tied in with Gypsies in Los Angeles. Here, I felt secure and excited about the promise of experiencing my biggest adventure yet.

CHAPTER 14

Solidly A Sailor

MY FIRST GLIMPSE OF the USS McKean 784 was overwhelming: it had a comparatively small size but a lethal potential to outrun any ship, decimate enemy submarines, deliver massive plunder to shore targets (aka batteries), protect US carriers by delivering air fire to oncoming enemy plane attacks, and provide a protective barrier from incoming torpedoes intended for carriers or other ships in harm's way. I got my pick of assignment: I was a gunner mate, in charge of the ship's big guns. I trained daily on the care, loading, and firing of the massive weapon.

"Mighty Mac" was the official nickname for the McKean, which made it sound personable and protective to its crew. I learned the recent history of "Mighty Mac" soon after coming aboard: It had been launched in 1945, following the surrender of Japan, and assigned to clearing Allied floating mines from the Japanese waters. In 1950, Mighty Mac had participated in the Inchon Invasion, the ground offensive operation against the North Korean Communists,

USS McKean 784 ("Big Mac")

and joined Task Force 72 in the Taiwan Strait with accompanying destroyers USS Frank Knox, USS Hollister, and USS Ozbourn, which culminated in battling Typhoon Clara.

The excitement I felt over my new post was curbed by intermittent seasickness, which came and went according to the ocean's surge for my first six months of sea duty.

The McKean rotated every six months between the US Naval Base in Long Beach, CA, and a six-month tour of Pacific destinations of crucial interest to the US. Each segment required daily work from the seamen from 6:30 a.m. to 8:00 p.m., during which time we did maintenance, assigned duty, and rotated on look outposts. We had breakfast at seven, midday meal at four, and dinner at eight on ship. Off duty after dinner, sailors had free time to play cards, socialize, read, watch navy-provided films, and write letters. We retired early due to exhaustion. Liberty, shore leave, took place in evening hours. We sailors were divided into two or three groups that alternated for days of leave. On some occasions, if the base was in the US, we got full weekend leave. Shore leave in foreign areas was restricted most often to one-day excursions.

Our six-month Pacific route included trips to Yokosuka Naval base in Japan (the home port from which the ship made its excursions); Inchon Harbor in South Korea; Sasebo, Japan; Kobe, Japan; Manila in the Philippines; Hong Kong and the Chinese mainland; and Okinawa. We were in constant rotation between these destinations, storing up on shells and food supplies from other ships and land bases in between. We were allowed to play baseball on the islands of Wake, Midway, and Clark Field in the Philippines, which was always a good time.

Off to China and the world

The six years that had elapsed since the ending of WWII had alleviated but not remediated the extensive damage done throughout Japan from bombing; the destruction was still evident despite rebuilding and reconstruction efforts of the Japanese, aided by financial support from the United States. People had been benefiting from massive food drops from America ever since the Japanese had finally signed their surrender aboard the Battleship USS Missouri, and this continued, but thousands of families were still living in caves. The Japanese women, in large part, were solicitous of the American GIs, while the Japanese men were clearly intimidated by and tried to avoid them. American GIs were hostile in their attitude toward the indigenous men but frequently married the women and brought them to the US.

Inchon, Korea, captured much of the Naval ships' attention during the early fifties as the US entered the fight on the side of South Korea. As US ground troops entered battle in support of the south, trying to stem the North Korean Communist invasion, the USS navy launched bombardments on North Korea—a months-long, repetitious assault. My ship, the USS McKean, intermittently delivered horrendous five-inch shells into South Korea to eliminate invading North Korean forces in coordination with the USS Missouri, which had the capacity to deliver more lethal shelling from fourteen- and sixteen-inch guns, indenting huge craters in the terrain.

The heated and violent shelling of the Korean Peninsula from the US Navy was loud, long, and intense. The McKean and other ships rotated their military maneuvers there for the duration of the war, from 1950 until 1953, when South Korea was established as independent by America's intercession. Throughout our time on the ship, we were indoctrinated with naval history—an essential element to preparing incoming sailors for involvement in war encounters.

A welcome respite from our strenuous, and often horrific, involvement in the war was shore leave on the Pacific route, which submerged us sailors in a panoply of history, foreign culture, travel, and entertainment.

We came to Hong Kong in 1953. I spent most of my time then with my friends Bat and Wilbur, both from California. Wilbur was a handsome, six-foot-five guy, and Bat—called that because he looked like Bat Man—was a fit, former high school wrestler. One day, we went into Hong Kong on leave. We took a Chinese-run water boat from our destroyer into the massive, hugely populated city, and grabbed a cab to the industrial area where all the Chinese merchandise was made and sold and which was known for making inexpensive suits. I was in the front seat with the driver, and Wilbur and Bat were in the back.

Wilbur and Bat had a system for making money. When we got to the bustling, frenzied streets of the merchants, one of my friends reached under the taxi driver's seat and took over $300 in Hong Kong dollars (about $30 in US money), from the small box where the driver had stashed his earnings. The Bat paid the driver with the money they had just stolen, and even gave him a tip. I really had to laugh in spite of the poor "slope's" unaware, smiling departure, which jingled my conscience a little.

In a tailor's shop, we split the take, which left us with about $100 Hong Kong bucks each, and then got measured for cashmere suits at a price of US $30 each, which were to be ready the next day. That accomplished, we went to the Star Bar, which was said to attract a lot of Eurasian women, also called White Russians—tall, blue-eyed, expensive prostitutes. We wanted to celebrate Wilbur's and my own promotion to third-class petty officers, which struck me as the right title, considering the petty ruse we had just pulled off.

At the Star Bar, we each found a beautiful Eurasian girl and pushed through Russian and English sailors, muscling our way toward the best spot at the center bar, clearly giving off an "I'll kick your ass" message to everyone.

A couple of hours of heavy drinking put us into a high and jovial, but aggressive, mood. Two wide-girthed, strong English sailors came up to Wilbur and asked him to buy them a drink. Wilbur bought them a beer each and was having a good time until one of them put his arm around Wilbur's neck in a playful move.

The English sailors had notoriously bad teeth and rotten physical hygiene, and their body odors were very offensive at close range. I was sitting next to Wilbur and caught the stink from under the English sailor's armpit, as did Wilbur, so he said, "Don't you Queen fuckers ever bathe? Put your arm down."

The English sailor grabbed his beer and threw it into Wilbur's face. With that, the fun changed to a different kind of fighting fun. We creamed the two Englishmen and three or four more English guys jumped in, with several Russians coming in on our side.

Before the fight, we had run up a bar bill of about US $140 because we were lavishly buying everyone drinks. After all the tables, bottles, and chairs were turned over, and the girls had fled, we slipped out to avoid shore patrol.

The owner came chasing after us for his money, and he was soon joined by a Chinese mob, all of them waving sticks and screaming to get us. We were running from a trampling. It was about midnight. We grabbed a cab and raced off for the dock, where we got onto a water taxi, still holding our beer bottles and laughing hysterically. We finished off our beers as the taxi wormed its way through about one hundred sampans.

One money collector on the water taxi tried to charge Bat US $30 to take us back to ship; he knew we had been into trouble. Bat grabbed him and threw him into the water. The other collector, terrified, dived into the water himself before Bat could come after him too. They were within easy swimming distance to the shore, they would just havee a waterlogged arrival.

Our driver was an old Chinese man whom I had to stand in front of to keep Bat from pitching him in too. The old man drove us to the carrier catwalk and we let him go without pay. We walked to our destroyer, laughing at all the excitement and fun we had.

The next day, Saturday, we got up to go pick up our cashmere suits, which we needed to visit Colon, a communist-controlled island city where naval uniforms were forbidden. We wanted to go there to buy some of the precious stones—rubies, sapphires, and apple-green jade—that the city was famous for.

We left our uniforms with the tailor, saying we'd be back to pick them up later at night. We took a water taxi and arrived to our promised land of jewels at 4:00 p.m., at which point we took a cab to the exact store Bat's dad, a jeweler, had told him about. Bat had learned a lot from his dad and knew what to look for and how to haggle over prices.

Three Chinese men greeted us at the store and took us into a crude-looking house that was connected to the store. One of them pulled out a shoebox from a cabinet and opened it up, revealing piles of jewels. Bat put on his jewelry inspection eyepiece and picked out all the jewelry he wanted to take to his dad.

Wilbur, Bat, and I put up US $1,200 each (which we had earned through our loan sharking business of lending money to sailors at 50 percent interest) for this venture. As our jewels were being packed, I spotted, on a high shelf, a one-foot-tall green jade Buddha and became determined to have it; I talked the guy into taking US $200 for it.

Our purchases made, we rushed back to Hong Kong, protecting our treasures, got our uniforms back on, and went nightclubbing, keeping our boxes of jewels and suits next to us in a box. Later, when we had to go back to the ship, we smuggled our jewels aboard.

Our next trip off ship took place on Christmas Day. This time, we went to a British Officers Club on a British base. We were called Yanks by the British, but we had a friendly, reciprocal relationship with the English servicemen. We ordered porterhouse steaks and turkey, and the food was superior. We paid our bill, saluted the officers in charge, and left, feeling we'd had an enjoyable and profitable visit to Hong Kong.

We arrived back in the States four weeks later. Upon arriving, we collected my car, which I had left at ship's docking area in Long Beach, and drove straight to Bat's dad's jewelry store in Santa Barbara. We got our investment back plus $3,500 each from his dad, but the Buddha I kept!

When I returned to Long Beach, I called my girlfriend, whom I'd met a month before shipping out and with whom I'd exchanged letters my whole time at sea. I gave her the Buddha as a gift.

Six months later, we broke up, and she kept the Buddha. I never saw it again, until I saw it—or an exact duplicate—on a TV auction thirty years later, priced at $20,000.

I replaced the girl many times over in the years to come, but I have forever regretted my foolish loss of that Buddha.

CHAPTER 15

Naval Leave: Juárez to Vallejo

THE USS MCKEAN DDR 784 Destroyer docked in Long Beach Harbor after a six-month tour of duty in the Far East, including Formosa (now Taiwan), Korea, Japan, the Philippines, Okinawa, and scattered small islands. After spending half of our tour time on ship and half on foreign lands for the last six months, it was exciting to hit US shores.

I was given a two-week leave. My friend Nick wanted to go with me to see my family in El Paso, primarily because he had heard so much about the rowdy, open town of Juarez, MX that bordered El Paso. He wanted to go with me to get the juice of Juárez and then he'd go on to his hometown, Dallas, TX.

We rode a Greyhound bus, got into El Paso in the early evening, and went straight to Juárez before dropping in on my family. The guy was crazy to get there, and I was more than ready for a "Juárez Review." We stored some cash in a locker at the bus station, washed up at the station, and, in our summer-white naval uniforms, hurried to get over the Juárez bridge because there was a 12:00 a.m. curfew for servicemen.

We rode the streetcar over the Juárez bridge and hit the first bar we saw: the well-known Mex-Tex Bar, which always had cheap booze and mariachis playing loud, ranch-style Mexican music with strong, emotional female and male singers. We danced and drank with a couple cute girls out to party, then went on to the Lobby, where Long John was playing hot rock music with his band on his saxophone. There, we drank and danced some more with two new girls from Midland, TX. The town was a constant party place, with young people everywhere in a celebrating frenzy, and this was a Friday night, so every place was packed.

We didn't even notice when midnight curfew passed that night. When we did finally remember the time, we knew we couldn't go over the border because we would be arrested for violating curfew. So we kept partying and took the girls we were hanging out with to the New York Bar, one of the many fabulous, high-quality but inexpensive restaurants in the area, for a superior dinner.

At dinner, Nick started playing a pinball machine. Drunk, he kept lifting the pinball machine, trying to make the ball go into the hole so he could score—when suddenly the top of the machine ripped off. We thought this was hysterically funny, until the owner let us know we had to pay him $75 to replace the machine. We only had $25 left, including what the girls chipped in, so he called the police, who, along with the bartenders, surrounded us. I still spoke and understood fluent Spanish, so when owner said I had been involved in breaking the machine also and the cops told us we owed double, $150, I stepped in.

Speaking in Spanish to the cops, I told them I was not involved in breaking the machine, which was verified by the bartenders and girls, and told them I had money in the bus station locker across the bridge. As they knew, I could not cross the border that night, having missed curfew, but I would go the next morning and come back with the money.

They handcuffed my drunk, and now very afraid, friend and drove him to the jail.

"I'll come get you in the morning, I promise!" I told him before they took him away. With nothing else I could do to help him then, I went back into the bar and ordered another round of drinks for about twenty-five cents each, and with my having both girls to myself, the fun picked up even more.

At about 3:00 a.m. I was so drunk I started throwing up in the bathroom. I was trying really hard to focus on what I was supposed to do for Nick, so I left the girls at the bar.

"I'll see you back here tomorrow night," I said, slurring my words. "I gotta go to the jailhouse to check on Nick!"

Outside, though, I started getting seriously dizzy, so I sat down on a curb, and I soon passed out, leaning against a telephone pole. At some point that night, I must have fallen over into the alley on my back, because I became conscious in morning's light to a poking feeling on my bare chest, which was pointed up at the sky. My throat was severely parched; I felt the blistering midmorning sun beating onto my face as I slowly opened my eyes and tried to focus, with a vaguely surfacing memory of being in Juarez.

A rooster's busy head was pecking on my chest. The sight of it scared me into full consciousness because it looked, in my dazed view, like a monster. I knocked it off of me and staggered to my feet, feeling faint and extremely thirsty, covered in mud, my jumper top and tie gone.

I went into the Guadalajara Bar, close to the jail, and called my good, old, dependable dad in El Paso, and he sent one of his fruit workers to pick me up and take me home to El Paso. Rescuing my friend was still my conscious objective, but I moved it way back in my mind for a later event. I fell into my old bed at home and fell asleep.

When I woke up at 5:00 p.m. that day I took a shower, put on clean clothes, and went in my dad's car to the bus station to retrieve our money from the locker. I drove to the Juárez jail and paid only $25 instead of the $75 they'd demanded before to get Nick out because I told the captain in charge that the police who had arrested him had taken all his money, which he readily believed because of the high rate of crooked cops in Juarez.

My friend was mad as hell at me for leaving him there so long, and looked very sad and demolished, which made me think he might have been the victim of some variety of abuse in jail.

"Why'd you leave me in there so long?" he demanded, furious.

"I'm sorry," I said, "there was nothing I could do! I got picked up for curfew violation, I was in jail all night too."

He believed me; I think that's the only reason our friendship survived the incident.

I took Nick to the bus depot and he went on to Dallas with probably no further desire to visit the infamous party city of Juarez. I hoped he'd be more put together when we hooked up again back on ship in two weeks.

I spent ten days in El Paso visiting all my friends and family. At the end of it, an El Paso friend who had a few days off from work offered to drive me back to Long Beach. Hank and Charles were still there, and I had a number to call them at when I got back there, so we headed west.

Upon arriving in Long Beach, we contacted Hank and Charles, then rented a flop house and got two huge jugs of wine.

"Be sure to wake me at 6:00 a.m. so I can get to my ship in time," I told the landlady. It was leaving Long Beach for Vallejo, CA the next day.

I woke up at 8:30 a.m. Angry, I confronted the landlady. "I said 6:00 a.m., remember?"

"I tried!" she cried. "You cussed me out and told me to get out."

I barely remembered doing that, but had a vague memory of something like that happening. *Shit.* My friend raced me to the dock, me panicking the whole way, and we arrived to see it sailing into the vast ocean, disappearing on the horizon.

I'd just made rank and knew I'd be busted soon enough anyway, so I turned myself in to the Shore Patrol on the Terminal Island Base, where they issued me traveling orders and gave me a bus ticket and money so I could meet my ship in San Francisco.

Upon arriving in San Francisco, I called my sister who lived there and she picked me up and took me to spend the weekend at their house so I could report to the ship on Monday in Vallejo. I got a week restriction as punishment, but I wasn't too upset: I really needed the rest.

CHAPTER 16

Kobe, Japan—Aika's Bar, Big Mac's End

ONE EVENING, MY SAILOR buddies Bob Hamilton and Lucky Fierro and I dressed in our tropical white uniforms and left the McKean, which had docked in Kobe, Japan after eight months sailing the waters around Korea.

As gunner's mate, I'd gotten the kicks of blasting off huge bellows of firepower inland and watching mountaintops in North Korea disintegrate. Now we'd docked after stays at Yokosuka and Sasebo and were rewarded with our seventy-two-hour leave, which we were not a minute late to start in Kobe.

Our anticipation of adventure was high as we headed for a downtown restaurant. Eight years had passed since WWII had ended, and much of the Japanese population was still homeless, many people living in caves. Construction and bombing cleanup was still underway.

At the restaurant, we ordered shrimp fried rice. It was served by the owner, an Anglo-looking woman who spoke

English. We asked her to sit with us as we ate so we could find out what she was doing in Japan.

She told us she had married a Japanese diplomat in Washington DC two years before war was declared by the US on Japan. She went to Japan with her husband and lived there for two years until Pearl Harbor, which had changed the way she was treated by the natives, but she'd stayed during the war, being very in love with her husband and their daughter. During the war, she'd been forced to work in the rice paddies with the peasants to support the Japanese war effort, even though her husband was held in prestige as a diplomat in Japan.

Every time American planes would drop bombs, the peasants would grab sticks and beat her in the rice paddies to vent their wrath against the US. Eventually, the beatings got so vicious that her husband managed to get her assigned to a safer job out of the fields. She told us she was writing her memoirs about her life as an American in Japan during the war, and that she still loved the US and was secretly glad we'd won, although she was now a Japanese citizen and would never express this sentiment to a Japanese person. She had learned to love the Japanese and their culture, of which her daughter was a part, and she was pained by her adopted people's suffering, especially by the bombing of Hiroshima and Nagasaki.

A few years after, in the late 1950s or early 1960s, I saw a movie that had all the many sequences and details of the many stories she told us that long afternoon. I felt sure the movie was her memoir come to life.

We became anxious for some fun and action. We left the storyteller and hailed a couple of rickshaws to get to the infamous Aika's Bar, where I'd several previous times visited a favorite girl named Susico. We plodded through the throngs of people we called "slope heads," a term born of the anger at the Japanese for the bombing of Pearl Harbor, but which dissipated and became extinct as the American and Japanese postwar cultures blended. They were all scurrying about like busy ants, friendly, even obsequious in their courting our friendship for a few yen, cigarettes, or whatever they could get off us.

There stood Aika's Bar, with American Western music pounding out the doors and filling the street. The Japanese bartender was wearing a cowboy hat and was singing "Home on the Range" in English delivered comically accented and hard to understand, but with a huge smile. We were infected with gut-deep laughter that carried through our high-spirited night.

"Mamasan," the head madam, found us at the bar, and I asked for Susico after I gifted her with a carton of cigarettes, which entitled me plentiful free drinks and half an hour with Susico, who had both beautiful features and body, a soft demeanor, and called me Burt Lancaster—plus her sexual indulgence was as imaginative as I wanted it to be, having no taboos against joyfully providing sexual activity to any guy the Mamasan had been paid by. We used to laugh about the blatantly solicitous open forum these girls would instantly and openly provide to please their customers. We were totally open and unscrupulous in our search for lustful fun. I always kept Susico for the whole evening; my friends also had their favorite girls. Together, we danced, talked, and laughed the night away. It was the mode of entertainment most in demand by the marines and sailors on shore leave, and we all eagerly jumped in.

This night, Mamasan said I'd have to wait a while and nodded toward Susico across the room, sitting on a marine's lap. I went over and grabbed her hand and took her with me without a word to the marine. She gleamed, showing she was up for it. We joined the table with my buddies and their girls and began our raucous good time, me reacquainting my hands with her body parts.

Through the music, I heard a thunderous yell from the marine whose lap I'd snatched Susico from: "I'm going to kick the ass of the biggest sailor in the room!"

"I guess you know that's you, Dave," Bob said. "Here we go again!"

The well-built, strong marine and his two buddies strutted over to us and grabbed Susico's arm as she leaned against me. He yanked her out of the way and issued the standard "Come on, you motherfucker" war talk. I grabbed my thick beer bottle and busted it over his head as I came out of my chair. He went flat on his back—and then the marine behind him kicked me in the testicles, which put me into such severe pain that I went unconscious.

I woke up on a bed to Susico putting ice packs on my excruciatingly painful groin. Bob said he'd beat the hell out of the kicker and the third marine had run out of the bar, leaving the first challenger marine still on the floor.

The Shore Patrol showed up after everyone had left and took me in an ambulance to a Japanese hospital staffed by Americans and Japanese. Mamasan and Susico had given a complete recounting of events, including names of marines.

The next day, I got out of my bed and into a wheelchair to go down the hall to the toilet, which seat was level with the floor, Japanese style. Lowering myself down and getting up was even more painful than it would have been on a western-style toilet.

I passed another guy in a wheelchair with a broken jaw and our brief eye contact told us we were each other's batterer.

"Aren't you the guy from Aika's Bar?" he asked.

"Yeah," I said, "are you the marine?"

"Yeah," he said, and we both started laughing.

"Look what happened to my balls," I said. "If I ever have kids, they'll all be retarded!"

We started joking, him saying *I* was retarded for hitting him in the head. We had a long talk over lunch—we ate in my room, so I could lie down—and agreed not to press charges against each other. We developed a close friendship during the two-day remainder of my stay there. I regret that we never ran into each other again, because he was a great guy with a sense of humor really synchronized with mine.

I also never knew if we ever shared Susico again. If we did, I never saw it.

Four years of international travel, intrigue, battle, immersion into foreign cultures, and military discipline culminated in the choice of reenlistment or rediscovery of civilian life. I opted for a new adventure as a civilian, leaving behind my naval brothers (in arms and in play), and returned to civilian life and my family.

Mighty Mac had been my home base and a source of adventure and friends who became my brothers for four years. I'd been onboard in 1955 when an underwater A-bomb test, Operation Wigwam, was conducted, during which we were all ordered to go below deck and not to look or venture on deck. One sailor who did go on deck undetected lost all his hair and was transferred and carried off ship by a rescue ship. The incident, by our commanding officer's incontrovertible instruction, was not to be talked about or again referenced by the crew. We were all compelled to sign a pledge not to divulge what we saw. Years later, however, it became public domain. In leaving service when I did, I just missed the upcoming trip to Singapore and to Melbourne for the Olympic Games being held there.

In December 1965, Mighty Mac's commanding officer wrote to the stateside families of the McKean sailors that the ship had completed a travel distance of 57,014 miles, more than twice the distance around the world at the Equator. Its expansive adventures became constant and included forays to Australia, New Zealand, and innumerable other destinations.

Mighty Mac was also sent to the Bay of Bengal during the Indo-Pakistani War, and had port calls in Hong Kong, New Guinea, American Samoa, and Pearl Harbor. She conducted generations of proud, brave, and seaworthy American naval personnel on world excursions, satiating the wander lust of many young men.

The burial of Mighty Mac was inglorious and injurious to all who served aboard her. She was given to the country of Turkey to be cannibalized for spare parts, then was sunk by Harpoon missile in July 1987. She now lies at the bottom of Antalya Bay off the Mediterranean Coast, not even in her own American waters. This was a sad ending to all us long-ago travelers.

The deep feeling of loss of close naval friends, incredible experiences, and adventure I felt as I severed myself from the Navy was lessened when I discovered, upon arriving home to El Paso, that my father was anxiously and excitedly planning a trip back into Mexico for the two of us. This promptly conjured up flash memories of the beautiful beaches and hospitable culture I had loved as a young boy. I couldn't wait to go back in time.

CHAPTER 17

Back to Mexico

MY NEW WHITE FORD convertible carried a film of dust from the Chihuahua desert as we pulled into a rundown adobe filling station. The usual stray dogs and a couple of barefoot boys ran up to greet my dad and me, hoping to collect a dime by pointing the way to the outhouse or carrying a soda to the travelers. The sun was blistering.

As I stepped from behind the wheel to stretch my legs, a dark little boy craned his neck to stare up at us and asked, "Can I get you a drink of cold water, señor, or a girl?"

I told the boy, in Spanish, to ask someone else, and gave him a few pesos. He looked like all the poor kids I had mingled with in my own boyhood years, doing business with my dad in Juarez, as well as every other poor boy I had seen in China, Japan, Korea, and the Pacific Islands: all desperate, but hopeful.

I loved the atmosphere of Mexico—the friendly people, the easy-moving life, the lack of any expectation of excitement or of better things to occur, just an earthy acceptance of simplicity that revolved around hard work, raising children, and cooking food.

There were few luxuries in Mexico. Even the small wealthy class did not have the luxuries that middle-class American citizens took for granted, like home heating. They built fires in their fireplaces, even in well-endowed mansions, and during the night, when the fires dwindled, they slept under deep, heavy blankets in the cold air. This crudeness appealed to me, and I reflected on the adverse reaction my mother, Gracie, had had to the same life. My innate nature and large physique seemed to make me inclined to blend with these rough surroundings.

This land, I knew, was my father's homeland, and partially, therefore, mine too. I was eager to experience it again, as I had been as a child when my Uncle Everado took me on the train to Mexico.

I remembered the sleek black horses, Cuervo and Indio, and all the uncles and their families that my dad and I were going to visit and stay with. My dad's six brothers all had wives and multiple children, and all were gracious hosts. They were enthusiastic to have their brother Joe, who had many times returned to Mexico to visit his family, arrive again with me, the nephew they had grown much attached to during my youthful two-year stay. I had made my First Communion in the Great Cathedral in Mexico City, and many of our family members had attended this most sacred ceremony.

As we closed the last gap of miles to the great and overcrowded Mexico City, my dad reminisced about his family's early settlement in Mexico, after their arrival from Spain, and how they attained great wealth and property in spite of the Revolution, which annihilated many people's land and money. All of my father's brothers had achieved success: one was a doctor, one had a pharmaceutical business, one was invested in the oil industry, and one owned a huge coconut plantation. All were educated and in the upper economic strata of the population. All were family-centered, and joyful to have their brother and nephew return.

Each night of our journey, my dad talked into the evening of his family and Mexico's traumatic history. He reminisced about the Revolution, and how he and his brothers had survived it. One of his brothers, Pepe, had been passionately committed to the cause and was a follower of Zapata. My dad told me the history of what he called "Pepe's Revolution."

My dad hated the Spaniards, although half his genetic lineage was only four generations away from its Spanish roots. The Spaniards had raped Mexican families—their bodies, their land, their food, and their culture—under the greedy grip of powerful dictatorship, which had led to an agrarian revolt among the landless sharecroppers who were forced to give all their produce to their rulers and were in a state of starvation.

My dad lived on a ranch in Mexico during this time, and he watched his brother, Pepe, grow into an avid revolutionary, joining Zapata's growing army. My uncle was known as Don Pepe the Furioso, and as "the Doctor." He was not a licensed doctor but was amazingly skilled at removing bullets and simple surgeries.

My dad's brother, Fortunado, was an actual medical doctor and cared for a lot of injured revolutionaries, to whose cause he was also committed. It was with Pepe and another brother, Simon, that my dad later hopped a freight train to Detroit, Michigan to join the work program at Ford School of Technology; Pepe did not want his two younger brothers involved in the fighting, and aspired for them to forge a new beginning for the family in the United States.

When Pepe got the deadly flu in Detroit and was taken back to the plantations in Mexico, he eventually recovered but lost interest in returning to America, as he became passionately involved in the Revolution. In his home at Uruapan, Michoacán, there was a major government fort. His friends and neighbors implored him to actively assume their area's leadership in the revolt against the *federales* sometime in 1921.

Six months later, the major revolt was over; Pancho Villa and his troops of agrarian volunteers had taken Mexico City. They quickly took over the government of the Mexican people. Communication being by horse, a span of time passed before all the federal troops learned that Mexico City had fallen to the rebels.

In 1955, on the beach in Zihuatanejo, Simon, Pepe, Benjamin, and my dad told their history to me and some of my cousins as we all roasted crabs. Simon now owned part of the beach, and all my uncles now had land and respectable businesses, homes, and large families in Mexico. Some had been awarded land by those grateful for their achievements in the people's fight, while some of their assets emanated from profits from a whiskey factory they had created. They were wealthy men.

As we all drank, we pumped Uncle Pepe to answer questions about his part in the Revolution. He said his left leg was six inches shorter than the right because he answered a summons by the *federales* to negotiate a peace treaty and turn in their arms as a peaceful surrender with the revolutionaries' terms met.

"The messenger told me they wanted to give me a horse," Pepe said, "that I'd earned it as a gift. So I took twelve soldiers with me but left fifty behind, in case it was a trap. I traveled eleven miles to the fort in Uruapan, Michoacán, and upon arrival we were all invited into the fort, where we surrendered our rifles and dismounted." He shook his head. "When a ridge of soldiers appeared above the fort with rifles aimed at us, we knew our fear of an ambush had come to pass. All my faithful soldiers were killed."

"How did you escape?" asked one of my cousins.

"I had seven bullets in my leg and left side; I thought I was done for. But a female cook who worked for the *federales* but was a revolutionary sympathizer dragged me to safety and tended to my wounds."

The fifty troops who waited behind surfaced quickly to rescue their leader and comrades and attacked the fort. The assault ended with vengeful killing of all federal soldiers and leaders and the hanging of the captain who'd arranged the fake treaty and murderous ambush. The colonel in charge of the fort tried to escape but ran into Pepe's charging revolutionaries and met his end.

The female cook doctored Pepe for a year. Someone removed the bullets and he healed with a stunted leg and limp. He married the cook and had three children.

Upon his death, Benjamin divided all his property equally among his twelve children, and Pepe and my father's other brothers did the same.

Some of the inheritors became alcoholics and squandered their good fortune, while an equal number invested well and became CEOs of emerging oil companies, or professional people and land owners with varying businesses.

As the Bible says, one son buried his talents, and the other went out and multiplied his.

Only my dad, Joe, kept his investment in America. He opened a fruit business in El Paso, Texas, and made good money, having workers haul and distribute fruit from Mexico to states like Colorado. He had a small office on Overland Street in El Paso, and it always filled with his close friends, all speaking Spanish. He often ate at a little Mexican restaurant, called Jefe's, for the fifty years he ran his business. As his son, I would see him take in wads of big bills in cash and also give a lot of it to people who were needy. If someone owed him money, he never pressed them for payment if they weren't doing well.

As his son, I traveled with him to Juárez and a few times to Colorado. In Juarez, I saw my old man respected, and saw how women were attracted to him. For a period of time he liked to drink too much and my mom would send me with him to watch him. I was about seven and loved being next to him. The women would bring me food or drinks and comment on my blond, curly hair. My dad and I went on long trips, driving fruit or just visiting his homeland. I now appreciated the great gift he had given to me when he had sent me there to live with Uncle Fortunado: in those two years, I'd learned the spirit, language, and culture of Mexico.

I was especially close to my dad and traveled with him often. We had long talks and laughs; he taught me history and about life and was a reasonable, very innovative, compassionate, and intelligent man, and, in his mustached, youthful, dapper days had been a handsome match for my mom. I was the closest and most constant companion to my dad and loved him above all others. When he died, my brothers gave me his wallet. I think of him daily and eventually went into business for myself because of him. I still hear things he said to me as we put miles on the highway or lunched often. In his older years after my dear mother died, I went to the old house in midtown and took him out to eat weekly.

Through my travels with my dad, I was gifted with a view and childhood experience of poverty—which, of course, taught me to make money on my own like my dad, or as I often called him, my "Jefe."

"David," he told me often, "never work for anyone; always be your own boss."

So I am, Jefe.

CHAPTER 18

A Stake in America—Now A Cop

MY TRIP WITH MY dad to Mexico would be carried in my heart forever, like a movie film, with all the characters and experiences indelibly in place. But I'd had enough of Mexico now, and we were driving the long road home to El Paso.

A month of relaxation in Mexico, lying half naked on a hammock in the sun, sucking coconuts on my uncle's plantation, and visiting all my excessively gracious relatives, had failed to remove the restlessness of my spirit. I had been out of the Navy two months.

My first month out, I'd combed El Paso for a job, and had come face to face with the same racism I thought I'd left behind.

"You're Mexican?" the man behind the desk asked as he scanned over my name on the application in front of him. "You don't look Mexican. Anyway, sorry, we don't hire Mexicans here."

No wonder so many Mexicans have their own miserable little businesses, I thought. *No one here will hire them.*

I had finally been accepted by the police department now, however—a job I thought of as ironic. Half of my good buddies with whom I had grown up were already in jail, having started with petty theft and graduated to the larger counts they got caught on. I had done my share of the petty offenses too, but had been spared a similar end by joining the Navy.

I got back behind the wheel. "Ready, Jefe?" I asked my dad.

He nodded and we pulled onto the highway to close the last miles between us and El Paso.

"Poor people," my dad reflected, referring to all Mexico that we were leaving behind.

"Hell Dad, its good here compared to the Orient," I said. "Every time our destroyer pulled into Incheon, we'd have to get out the water hoses to beat the people off. They'd swarm out like flies on their sampans, little wooden junk boats, and surround the ship to grab up the garbage we'd dump overboard. I remember one time I saw a Chinese girl lie right down on the floor of one of those little junkies and pop off a baby as everyone stepped over her, paying no attention, and the junks were banging into each other, fighting for the garbage and dodging the water hoses. Then she wrapped the baby up, stood up, and got right into the hassle for garbage. I couldn't believe it. Women in the States lay in bed for days after springing a kid."

"Yes, David," my dad responded, "but those people don't live long that way, especially the women. They die early."

"You know," I continued, "they just don't value life like we do, Dad. One time I saw a little girl about four years old floating naked, face down in the water, between the sampans, and no one even fished her out, they just went about their business. Hell, you think the beggars here are bad—they've got eight- and nine-year-old girls propositioning sailors over there. These poor bastards have it hard just making it day to day."

We kept talking as the day cooled and we neared El Paso. I felt very close to my dad—Jefe, meaning boss, or the old man, as I had always affectionately called him. This trip had been a perfect reunion.

I would report to the El Paso Police Department the next day, and I was ready, hoping to regain some of the excitement I'd left behind in the navy.

I adjusted my tie in the mirror. I 'd always taken pride in the way I looked in my Navy uniform, and this police uniform looked about as sharp. My belt, badge, and shoes were shined. My energy was focused on my new agenda. I was serious in my commitment, while also knowing I would not allow my nature of extracting every ounce of joy, humor, and excitement from life to diminish. I reflected on what decisions I would be called on to make and what tactics I would need to learn to meet the job requirements and just decided to take it all as it came and proceed with good sense.

I was not a naïve rookie. I'd been around the world and witnessed the most sordid side of people. I'd been in Juárez jails and hopped freight trains around the country since I was twelve. I'd learned to con the hobos by the time I was fourteen and had never really gotten the bad end of anything. I'd been stuck in a freezing freight car for two days with no food at the age of fifteen, and worked like a peon in the canneries and on the docks in California—damned back-breaking labor, but I hadn't minded: it had been an outlet for my intense energy, and my biceps had measured eighteen inches when the summer was over.

I pulled myself up to my full height and strapped on my gun. This job couldn't be any more challenging than anything else I'd been involved in; I was ready for whatever was to come.

I blended in easily and immediately with the rough humor and rank language that the patrolmen and officers spewed off like a badge of toughness at my new job. The captain took an immediate liking to me, as I did to him. I had learned to adjust my tone to any situation and so showed no expression of amazement or disapproval at the inefficiency and outright loose-ass way the outfit was run, although I felt amazement at the blood-smudged wall of the interrogation room and the cigar-puffing officers hunched over a craps game in the back room.

Whenever porno movies were confiscated, half the PD had an all-night party watching the films. A good number of the old, up-through-the-ranks-officers were booze hounds who showed up to work with a bad disposition, bad breath, and "booze fever." I watched a couple of confessions being extracted from some poor Mexican peons. The extraction was swift and brutal, and accounted for the blood smudges on the wall.

One thing was evident; no one gave the police any static. *How the hell do these guys get the nerve to arrest anyone?* I wondered. *They're breaking every law on the books.* I knew early that the game was politics; there certainly was no merit system involved in making your way up. Any idealistic rookies on the upward climb got a hand in the face and were kept down.

Luckily, I neither possessed nor showed such idealism. I would adjust. At the station, I listened to the war tales, gossip, and back biting and thought, *These guys are about as professional as a bunch of Hong Kong hookers. Hell, the hookers are more professional, at least they're straight out about what they're doing and they know how to do it well.* On the street, I was much more understanding and sympathetic than my colleagues. I was not an easy push, but I felt sorry for a lot of the poor men I had to arrest—winos, or vagrants sleeping on the street curbs or hanging around stores and bars, making the area seem unsafe to passersby.

One day, I picked up a hysterical teenage Chicano who panicked at being caught puffing a reefer while hanging around a corner trying to look cool; rather than booking him, I dragged the pathetic kid home to his mother in the "Segundo Barrio" or "Second Ward," a poverty-stricken tenement area, where one downstairs bathroom for all 200 occupants was the average. The people lived nine to twelve to a room, sleeping on the floor. Fear of contracting a disease or bumping into a junkie or pervert kept many of them from using the common bathroom, so they kept a large metal wash tub in the corner of the room that served as a toilet and was dumped periodically.

I climbed up the dark stairs and knocked at the door, which the youngster had pointed to humbly as his own. The harassed, fat woman looked horrified seeing a policeman with his hand on her boy's shoulder.

I stepped into the door, delivering the boy in front of me. "Señora," I began in fluent Spanish, "I picked him up puffing grass. You've got to keep him off the streets and watch what he's doing."

I realized the hopelessness of my suggestion even as I was making it. I saw the newborn baby sleeping in an open drawer of a broken-down wooden chest, and the quiet, expressionless faces of the seven little kids sitting on the only bed in the room staring up at me as I talked and their mother listened nervously. I realized the implausibility of the woman, with all these kids, keeping an eye on anyone. No wonder the boy stayed away from that stench-filled, one-room dump. As I spoke, I felt something drop onto my shoulder and I instinctively and hurriedly flipped off. It was a lively black roach, most probably from an impressively large roach den. Looking up, I saw the corner over my head pulsating with a swarm of them.

"Good Lord, lady, at least clean this place up," I told the mother, and left.

Many of the people I encountered on the streets fell into a different category: the pushers, kid molesters, and mouthy knife carriers. These I took no static from; I met any outright aggression from them with a heavy hand. I was glad to shed walking the beat downtown when I was assigned to a patrol car, which allowed access to a much larger area to police and which put me in a position to be called to assist in any instance where added cops were called in to help other cops involved in arrests of criminals or aiding citizens in emergencies or in danger. The Border Patrol and Fort Bliss solicited our help in picking up illegal immigrants, referred to as "wetbacks"—implying they had waded through the Rio Grande River, which was the designated border between the US and Mexico, to enter the US. Many of them did exactly that, and others just walked, without being apprehended, across the Santa Fe Bridge on the El Paso–Mexico Border, or across two free bridges in a more remote area. The Border Patrol desperately needed help dealing with the influx of these immigrants and paid cops two dollars for each wetback we picked up and delivered to a holding jail (from there, they were released back into Mexico and were sometimes flown to Mexico City). Fort Bliss also paid cops twenty-five dollars for every army deserter we picked up.

The immigrants were easy to spot by their usually shabby dress, their location around the uninhabited border areas, and their look of abandonment. Deserters were easy to spot as they could usually be found around highways hitchhiking in civilian clothes but wearing those telltale army boots and crew haircuts. We checked their ID and took them to Fort Bliss, where, once their status as a deserter was confirmed, the military police took over.

My car patrol partner was an Anglo. In the next couple years, I was to learn I would rather have a Mexican for a partner. These Mexican cops were from lower-income backgrounds, which meant they were raised close to the streets and had taken their blows; they knew how to confront a street fight and were prudent but unintimidated. The Anglo cops seemed to have had a more sheltered upbringing and had not been exposed to much street hassle, and in a tight spot, sometimes you couldn't count on them for common sense or guts.

CHAPTER 19

Death at A '50s Drive-In

I WAS IN A meeting with about forty cops to honor Willie's promotion to detective at the El Paso Police Department in 1957. He was a car patrolman like me, and had just taken the step up that I would take a year later. He called me over and gave me his patrol jacket because we were good friends, having worked as partners frequently.

Willie had talent for remembering any series of numbers, which meant he spent every minute looking for stolen cars' license plates. "Willie," I'd told him once, "I hope you make that detective rank you put in for, 'cause I'm sick of looking for cars!"

There were a bunch of "joy riders" (car thieves who stole cars for rides and ditched them) in the area. There were also serious crimes happening consistently on our El Paso–Juárez border town that I'd rather have been scanning for, however.

After the ceremony, I left with my new partner, who was a trick shot artist—he could shoot a quarter out of the air—a good partner to have for a shoot-out.

A month after Willie became detective, on a cold October night, my partner and I were on night patrol around 8:00 p.m. I was wearing Willie's jacket (it was warmer than my own) when we got a call that a Safeway grocery store across the street from the Pershing Movie Theatre, in midtown, had been robbed by two white gunmen just thirty minutes before the call went out. The car description was a new, black Lincoln Continental.

We were close to the El Paso drive-in theater when another call came in over our radio. It was Willie, saying he and his partner had the two gunmen in custody at the drive-in; he said he had them handcuffed and needed no help and that he was located near the concession stand—and then we heard a blast of shooting.

We rushed into the drive-in, spotted the black Lincoln, and jumped out of our car and ran toward it.

As soon as we were out of our car, another patrol pulled up, a cop we knew called Conejo, also jumped out and ran toward the Lincoln. He was shot four times immediately, and dropped to the ground. He miraculously survived the four bullets. I was running with my partner as he approached the detective car and we both saw Willie at the steering wheel, his head thrown back and a huge bullet hole in his left eye. The other detective was not in sight. My partner plugged the two robbers in their heads where they sat in the backseat of the car, killing them instantly.

I opened Willie's car door and pulled him out as he incoherently mumbled. I held him in my arms, both of us on the ground, until the ambulance arrived. He clutched fiercely at his jacket, which I was still wearing. I'd only been holding him about ten seconds when his head fell limp and his breathing stopped. I helped put him into the ambulance, but I knew he was dead. I was too stunned to feel any immediate emotion.

The detective we couldn't see at first came up to us then. He had been hiding behind a car, waiting for help. He said he had been in the front passenger seat next to Willie. The robbers were handcuffed with only one pair of cuffs because he and Willie didn't have a second pair; the cuffs were between the two men in the backseat, one arm of each man in a cuff, leaving the prisoner on the right side of the backseat with a free right arm and the prisoner on the left side of the backseat with a free left arm.

"I got out of the front passenger seat and opened the back door behind it, where the captive with the free right hand was sitting," he told us. "I was planning to get some information from the guy; I had a pad and pen in my hand. But when I leaned in to talk to them, the man with his left hand free reached over, grabbed my necktie, and yanked me into the car, and the guy closer to me grabbed my gun. Willie heard the commotion and turned around, and the guy shot him right in the face." He looked down. "I pulled myself free and ran for safe cover. Without my gun, I couldn't engage with them."

The Chief and a hoard of first responders and cops flooded the scene. We told onlookers to go back to their parked cars, where they had been watching the big-screen movie, at the front of the drive-in theatre.

The movie never even stopped while all this went on. The spectacle over, life at the movies went on.

As everyone wrote reports and exchanged information, I felt Willie's death grip on my jacket as he was raised off the ground onto the stretcher and slid into the ambulance. Even in death, his hand had clutched the jacket; I'd had to pull his fingers from their grip to release him to the ambulance. I'd watched the ambulance take him away, knowing I'd never talk to him again and thinking, *Willie, in one month you made detective, got married, and got murdered.*

The trunk of the Lincoln held an estimated $350,000 in cash and a box of a dozen Rolex watches and jewelry. The investigation discovered their second car, a new Cadillac, parked at the downtown Del Camino Hotel. Their specialty was robbing grocery stores in various cities on Fridays, which were the stores' biggest cash-intake days. The robbers both had prison records. Both were in their middle-to-late twenties. Willie was thirty. I continued to wear his jacket, and frequently, for a long time, could still feel his grip as the life slipped out of him.

The patrol car cop's unpredictable daily experience ranges from severe and extremely dangerous for the cop, his compadres, and civilians, to dull, routine, and tedious. The routine part can be very misleading, however, as a seemingly simple house call can sometimes prove to be a death summons.

CHAPTER 20

A Shot in the Face

IN 1958, AT AGE twenty-four, I was on patrol with Eddie Maestas in downtown El Paso when we got a domestic disturbance call at 316 Chihuahua Street. We arrived and knocked on the door of the small house from which the call had come. A lady in about her late forties came to the door and, sounding very frightened, poured out her frantic story: Her ex-husband had come to her house with a bayonet and threatened her when he saw she had another man living with her. She didn't know he had been released from prison (which he'd been sent to for murdering the woman's previous boyfriend five years earlier). After brandishing his bayonet and raging at her uncontrollably, she'd called the police and he'd taken off running.

"You go that way," I told my partner, pointing in one direction around the house. "I'll circle around the other way and meet you."

I jumped a four-foot-tall rock wall fence to access the backyard, and as I looked under the iron stairway, which had open spaces between each step, I saw him hiding with a gun aimed at my face just two feet away. Within the same second that I spotted him, he pulled the trigger—and his gun jammed. I frantically moved backward, raised my gun, lowered myself to the ground, and fired off about three rounds. He simultaneously fired three or four rounds back from his .32 automatic. He came out toward me as we cross fired at each other, both erratic and moving fast to avoid one another's bullets, and then he bolted into the house—where the woman and her boyfriend were huddled—through the back door.

I got up and jumped the wall back to my patrol car for cover as the man reappeared halfway out of the back door of the house with a rifle pointed to fire, looking for a target. My partner came racing toward the back of the house just then, headed for the shooter's direct line of fire.

"Get back to the patrol car!" I screamed, realizing that Eddie had not spotted the shooter and was within the guy's range.

Eddie veered away from the shooter and toward the car. When he got there, I threw him the keys so he could get on the car radio and call for help. I, meanwhile, positioned myself behind another car, closer to the aim of the shooter, at which time I felt blood oozing from my side. I would later realize that one of his bullets had simply grazed me; then, however, in the frantic focused fire exchange, I thought I could have taken a bullet in my side.

Still crouched behind the patrol car, I reloaded as fast as I could as the shooter walked toward me, firing his rifle. I peeked above the rear fender of the car, got a good aim at his rifle arm with my .357 Magnum, and fired my full five-cylinder of bullets on him, trying to bring him down. I hit his left wrist, but he managed to dodge back into the house.

I was vaguely aware that a small group of people who had just disembarked from a Greyhound bus at the nearby terminal were filming the gunfight. All was silent through the bullet storm; there were no screams, no voices, just the sound of firing bullets.

After he reentered the house, the shooter and I quickly reloaded and he reappeared. My partner was still busy calling for help. The shooter fired two shots through the windshield of the car I was standing behind; for a few seconds I was a direct target for him, but he missed again.

Three police cars drove up and out rushed three cops with rifles who quickly took refuge behind an apartment across the yard, where they had a good vantage point on the shooter. One had just gotten on top of the roof when the shooter stepped into full view by the back door, with rifle aimed, screaming, "*Matame!*"—meaning, "Kill me." We obliged with a determined fury to save our own lives, nailing him with a cross fire of bullets: six from my Magnum, and one definitive shot from Tom Darnel's shotgun from the roof, which blew off the shooter's head.

When the firing stopped, the woman who had called the police cautiously stepped out of the door and said vindictively and in relief, "Que bueno." Her words carried an emphasis we all felt. She walked quickly back into the house, where her boyfriend was still hiding.

My partner rushed over. "You're covered in blood," he said, concern on his face.

Only then did I realize I had not one but two bullet creases on my side. I was numb and feeling no pain, but a surreal ecstasy that I had escaped death filled me. I was in shock, kind of paralyzed. The adrenaline rush was violent and hard to subdue. Returning to calm, normal thought waves was a struggle. All of us cops in arms together felt it. The shock allowed us to seem normal, and we moved robotically. Shaking that surge would be a long process.

I thought the pursuit and kill had lasted an hour, but it had in fact consumed only twenty minutes—validating the idea that time stands still in a crisis. I was frozen in a nightmare; it was like dreaming of trying to breathe under water.

The coroner came to pronounce the shooter dead and remove his body. The filming group from the bus dispersed, and one of them approached me.

"This reminds me of the shootouts in the Old West, like OK Corral," he said. "It was fantastic and I got it all on tape."

Our captain told Eddie and me to take the day off. The two of us had only gone two blocks before Eddie told me to pull over to a nearby liquor store. He gingerly stepped out, and returned five minutes with a pint of Jim Beam whiskey. We both took a shot before we drove off.

We never saw the film—but that night, my picture was in the *Herald Post Newspaper*, about an 8x10 photo of me in my uniform, taken at the scene. It jolted through my thoughts that it could have been a dead cop picture. I could not understand why I did not die after having been fired on close and directly by at least ten or fifteen rifle and .32 automatic pistol bullets. I felt God around me.

A couple days later, while I was still calming down and trying to accept the trauma, knowing that the experience was something I could expect to encounter again in my job, I got a call from the shooter's brother at the police department.

"You killed my brother," he said flatly. "I'm going to shoot you whenever I see you, you motherfucking son of a bitch."

With that, he hung up. I immediately went and got a warrant for his arrest, which was easy, as he was a well-known Smelter Town burglar who already had warrants for his arrest.

It's fearsome to have a death threat hanging on you from the brother of a guy who already did his best to kill you. Eddie went on vacation right afterward, so I was quickly assigned a new partner, Ted Frazzer, who happened to be a good friend of mine—we had served in the Navy together. We went together to pick up the warrant and tracked the brother down in Smelter Town.

We spotted him sitting on his porch. At the sight of our patrol car, he took off running into a neighbor's house; we pursued on foot and ran right in through the front door after him in very hot pursuit. A lady was sitting in a rocking chair, looking afraid. She pointed to the bathroom down the hall. He had left the door open, so we went into the empty-looking room with guns drawn. I flung back the shower curtain, and we found him curled up in the bathtub.

We grabbed and arrested him and booked him into jail, where he stayed until he was transferred back to prison.

While all this was happening in El Paso, my brave partner in the shootout, Eddie, was enjoying his family time, away from death and murder, at Big Bend National Park. He was shooting the rapids with his three sons, ages about four, five, and eight, when the boat flipped and dumped all three boys into the water. I was told that Eddie pulled them each out of the water, one at a time, and pulled them to shore safely—but while trying to retrieve his boat with his last determined bit of energy, he disappeared into the water before his family's eyes and never came up.

Everything for me at this point was a whirlwind of traumatic stress and convoluted thought. I kept trying to reorganize and make sense of my life again—trying to stabilize my mind—but the news that my dear friend had drowned just a few weeks after the shootout was too much to process. I thought about the shootout, and him, and our shot of whiskey to digest our survival, painfully and unrelentingly. Bizarre thoughts and emotions swirled in my head. Every thought that sprang into my twisted mind as I tried to understand the horrific events that had just occurred was muddled and fruitless. All I knew for sure was that I would miss Eddie forever.

For the next two or three years, I would often see, in my sleep, a gun pointed at my face—sometimes the gun under the stairway, sometimes the rifle zinging bullets into the car windows, searing my side. It was not a vague dream but a reliving of the assault. I would see the gun, and the bullet ejecting right into my face.

In 1959, I got a simple domestic call about a girl who had caught a Peeping Tom hanging from the rooftop, in the dark, peering into her bathroom window as she took her evening shower. I responded and recognized the house when I arrived as the same one I 'd been to two years before, in 1957, to take a complaint about a girl, age seventeen, who had been robbed by a young Mexican boy who'd pointed an object, supposedly a gun, through her car window as she was exiting a grocery store parking lot. She'd given him all her money—all she'd had was a bit of change—and her father had called the police after she returned home and told him the story.

The area this family lived in was typically and securely 1950s in demographics and design—not elegant, but simple, clean, with embellished lawns and foliage. Most of the homes were two- or three-bedroom dwellings, with a carport and asbestos siding or brick veneer exteriors. The population was exclusively middle-income families, typically stay-at-home moms and working fathers.

At that first visit, I had told the father that I needed to interview the young lady involved. She had not wished to cooperate, as she was getting ready for a date, but upon coercion from her father, she'd come out to talk to me. I'd filed the report and returned to my evening shift with a lingering impression of her beauty.

On this second visit, I again asked the father to bring the girl to speak to me. She came into the small living room, annoyed, as before, at having her preparation for a date night interrupted. She was beautifully and seductively dressed in a green velvet dress that enhanced her wide green eyes; her makeup accentuated her exquisite beauty. She sat down, impatiently at first, until she looked directly into my eyes—at which point her aloofness subsided and she became very slightly seductive in her demeanor. I could see I had her attention.

I questioned the girl only briefly that night, and was interrupted again and again by her watching father's frequent and overly helpful intrusion during that time. I summated my report and left with reluctance.

I told my partner that night that I had just seen the most beautiful girl in El Paso. This was a girl I wouldn't forget.

CHAPTER 21

Reconnecting and Disconnecting

I HAD BEEN OUT of the navy for a few years now, but I was still getting reacquainted with family members whom I had seen or heard from only sporadically during my years of service.

One of these family members was my younger cousin Ralph—who, to what he considered his unbeatable disadvantage, had been born with an obvious physical claim to our Mexican ancestry, with none of the Anglo traits people saw in me. I had only my name to get around; Ralph, however, with his brown eyes and hair and conspicuously dark complexion, was a frequent target for racial slurs.

In a futile attempt to negate his Mexican identity, Ralph had refused to learn to speak a word of Spanish, while my closeness with my dad and my two-year stay in Mexico as a child had made me fluent in the language.

As a young adult, Ralph had enlisted as a soldier in the US military, which had allowed him to escape the racial intimidation of El Paso. In the armed services, he created a new identity, and began to see in the mirror the reality of what everyone, especially girls, had always seen—that he was strikingly handsome.

Ralph and I were both large, even as boys; being the older cousin, I'd always had the extra inches and weight necessary to put a fight in my favor, but that hadn't stopped Ralph from giving into his temper and exchanging blows with me when we were kids and he came to visit.

My mom's mother, the widow of my mom's deceased but never forgotten father, Lloyd, had moved in with her and my dad so soon after they were married that we couldn't remember the house without her. She was no joyful addition; Grandma was sick often and depressed constantly. The medicine she took for her unidentified illness made her mentally un-alert. In her later years, she often wandered off aimlessly, and had to be chased after and found.

Grandma's hostility to me was open and even aggressive. My whole bearing and appearance had always reminded her of Lloyd—she often fantasized vocally that I could even be Lloyd reincarnated—and she seemed to want to remake me, to keep me from growing into the same self-centered star that, she complained, her dead husband had been. Lloyd had also had the outgoing personality she claimed to see and strongly disapprove of in me, and she found it just as dangerous and repugnant in her grandson as she had in her husband. True, as a young woman she had been totally infatuated, like everyone else, with Lloyd's magnetism and zest, but she had reassessed his nature in her first married years with him as being undisciplined and insensitive to anyone's needs but his own, and his zest for life as an excuse to follow his whims off to an unnecessary enlistment to war, leaving her and their young children and abandoning his newly hatched but growing medical practice. Many, including her, considered his actions not patriotic but stupid, and other available young doctors quickly picked up his abandoned patients. He returned at the end of his service to reestablish his life, and found it a difficult task.

Eventually, with Lloyd gone, Grandma became my mom and dad's burden, which spurred my dad to increasingly spend more time out of the house and at his fruit business. Luckily, he took me with him. That was the start of my indoctrination into entrepreneurship, and my lifetime closeness with my "Jefe."

I grew up in an atmosphere of extreme racial prejudice against Mexicans. The language and culture of Mexico was fused into the El Paso population, but that didn't keep the stigma of racial prejudice against the Mexican immigrants and American-born Mexicans at bay. Joining the military gave us a distance from the heavy prejudice, a secure place, an income, self-esteem, and often job skills we could use to get civilian jobs upon our release from service. Those who, like me, had one Mexican parent and one Anglo parent often spent their life riding the fence—seeking their identity and trying to blend the two cultures, which often had completely different histories, languages, religions, and cultural norms.

I, however, was pressed as a child into learning to negotiate both cultures simultaneously. Thus I grew up with no feelings of imbalance, but rather a growing feeling of mastery and adeptness, using both cultures to my advantage.

Ralph sank into the worn-out sofa at my dad's house, watching me polish my police shoes with my foot propped against the sofa arm. I was in uniform and ready to start my shift.

Ralph was in civilian clothes, enjoying his ten-day furlough sans uniform.

"What're you going to do when you get out of the military?" I asked, glancing sideways at him while still giving full concentration to shining my shoes.

"Look for a job, like you did," Ralph said.

"Shit," I said flatly, "you know what I got when I went looking: a shoe in the ass. Why don't you come on the PD?"

"I'm thinking about it," Ralph said. "You seem to love the job; I like that you always seem eager to get to it. Your life seems fun."

"It's not always fun," I said seriously, "but you're right, I do love the job."

"Yeah, seems that way," Ralph said, nodding.

The military had done him good. Now he was ready to resume his life—but if he did in fact become a policeman, he'd be picking work that could be more dangerous than any peacetime military position.

I felt well set in my life: I had a slew of friends, girls were plentiful, and I liked my job. Some days were routine, but most days involved epic, challenging situations involving a variety of criminal activity: trafficking of or overdoses on drugs, rape, breaking and entering, prowlers, murder, battering, domestic violence (which could be the most dangerous situation to respond to), missing kids, gang fights, assault with deadly weapons, robberies, kidnapping, and mentally ill persons engaging in a delusional and threatening activity (which usually involved a standoff where we tried to disarm and apprehend the person). Auto, motorcycle, and even bicycle accidents gave up numbers of tragically injured or dead citizens to attend to. A quiet day could turn violent instantly, creating an adrenaline rush that hung on long after your shift ended.

Ralph sat quietly as memories of past police encounters raced through my mind in colorful, intense splashes.

August 3, 1961, I was working the night shift, on until 6:00 a.m. Around 3:00 a.m., my partner and I got a call to rush to the airport: a hijacking was in progress.

We sped to the El Paso International Airport and drove onto the tarmac. There were several FBI agents on hand, and the head agent had already contacted FBI Director J. Edgar Hoover, who, in turn, had advised President Kennedy of the situation. The President had instructed Hoover not to allow the plane to leave.

The plane had by this point been on the tarmac for hours and the hijackers, a thirty-eight-year-old man and his sixteen-year-old son, had taken hostages. This was the first plane hijacking in the history of the US, and the President was not about to let it succeed. Together, I and several other cops shot out the two front tires of the plane. I was using my .357 Magnum, but the real demolishment of the tires occurred when machine guns were brought out and given to the FBI agents on scene, who seared the tires and ensured the plane was going nowhere.

Once we'd disabled the plane, two FBI agents went up to the entry door and opened it. They encountered little resistance from the unsuccessful perpetrators; in no time, they had handcuffed them, extracted them from the plane, and released the passengers.

This whole experience was more like a military maneuver than a police incident, although we cops on the scene were very engaged containing the boundaries and safeguarding all the people in the area, as we had no assurance the hijackers would not make a violent move.

After eight cliffhanger hours, I got to go home and sleep.

The plane hijacking was a major national incident involving the highest level of government attention and was resolved without one of us getting a scratch—unlike a bar fight we were called to one night, which proved to be a life-threatening challenge.

On this occasion, my partner and I were called to the Red Barn, a local bar and dance establishment frequented by soldiers, cowboys, college kids, and lots of women wanting to dance and meet guys. The fight was called in as a "disturbance," but it was more like a riot. When the two of us stepped through the doorway, we heard women screaming and men yelling over the loud music, and saw about four or five men and women alike fist fighting while the crowd cheered.

I grabbed the first guy I saw, who had a woman on the ground and was socking and smacking her. I yanked him up, and he turned toward me and gave me a sock in the face. The woman who he'd been whacking jumped up on my back, grabbed my hair, and held on to it as she scratched my face and tried furiously to pull out my hair; her boyfriend, meanwhile, came at me again. I felt like I was in a fight with wild chimpanzees.

I flipped the woman roughly off my back—losing some of my hair in the process—and leveled her boyfriend to the floor with a fist to the head. I cuffed the man as the woman's friends grabbed her to extract her from the fight. The woman was drunk, and her friends begged me to let them take her home instead of arresting her. I agreed, but took the guy in for jail time.

My partner had his own hassle going with other drunk and abrasive patrons, but as soon as they registered that arrests were being made, they all stopped fighting.

We both agreed later that the hijacking had been way easier.

A year prior to the hijacking, I received another call involving an aircraft—on this occasion, a naval seaplane making an emergency landing at Ascarate Lake, which was woefully inadequate in size to accommodate the seaplane.

I arrived at the lake alone and was relieved to see only a few people meandering around the area; there was no crowd control to handle. Still, I knew that if the pilot missed the lake, the damage the plane would cause would be catastrophic.

After waiting for a short while, I heard the plane approaching at a speed of what I estimated to be 100 to 150 miles an hour or more. Given that rate of speed, the lake really appeared too small for the plane to land in without crashing into the shore on the other side.

It was a small plane; only a pilot and copilot, no passengers, were inside. It hit the water mid-lake with great force and careened toward the lake edge in what looked like an inevitable head-on crash, but the savvy pilot reversed his engines, causing the plane to lurch and quickly lose its speed. It stopped abruptly, landing with a great splash, just about ten feet short of the lake's edge. Onlookers fully expected an explosion, as it so speedily had raced toward the edge, and many people were making the sign of the cross when it stopped just short of impact. I was the only cop there to maneuver and control the crowd.

Very quickly, a naval rescue team arrived with a small boat, which they used to evacuate the two pilots. The plane sat in the water all night. The next day, a naval crew returned, fueled and placed jet boosters on each side of the plane and boarded the pilots. The plane made an easy take-off on the wings of Lady Luck.

David Suarez was known to the PD as an aggressive perpetual drunk, twenty-six years old, who always fought the arresting officer. He was frequently sentenced to thirty days in jail for drunk and disorderly abusive conduct but was extremely friendly, cooperative, and likable when he was sober. We made him a trustee at the police firing range, assigning him the task of cleaning the area and picking up fired shells, each time he served his thirty days. He was obliging and appreciated the respite from the cell.

During his frequent arrests, Suarez was sometimes battered by the arresting police, as he never cooperated and attacked them viciously. There were no tasers then; we had only our guns or our night sticks.

One day, Suarez saw that a patrolman had left his key in the ignition of his car at the firing range and he took off in the patrol car. The dispatcher made a general all points call to all cop cars, and Suarez heard the call come in. He picked up the mike in the car and went on a verbal rampage, calling us "*pinche putas*" and cursing out every sergeant he knew, as well as the chief of police and a number of local judges.

After a few hours, cops found the car crashed into an ice maker at a train yard. Suarez had hopped a train to Los Angeles.

One year later, another detective and I were in Los Angeles, headed to lunch, and we randomly asked an LA cop about Suarez. We told him the whole Suarez saga, and he asked me what the escapee looked like. I pointed to a guy approaching us from a distance and said, "He looks like that guy there."

The guy I was pointing to kept getting closer, and as he passed by, he looked right into my eyes.

"David Suarez!" I cried in amazement, stepping toward him.

He looked right at me from inescapable close range and knew he was had. "*Chinga tu madre*," he sneered (which in Spanish is a vile insult to one's mother), but he put up no resistance as we grabbed him.

It turned out that he had been working at a parking lot across the street from where we apprehended him. We cuffed him and took him to the LA jail for extradition back to El Paso. In the end he rode back to El Paso in the backseat of a police van, handcuffed to a bar. The US Marshall told us he behaved well and he was fed hot dogs on his trip.

Suarez got a year in county jail. I quit the PD before he was released, and I heard nothing more about him after that. He was a friendly, funny guy when he wasn't drunk or high on marijuana. I hope things worked out for him.

While on car patrol, my partner and I spotted a car parked in the desert at four o'clock in the afternoon with the back door open and what seemed to be part of a body protruding from the backseat. We rapidly approached and found an older man, his pants down below his knees, lying on top of a little thirteen-year-old girl, making sexual thrusting motions with his hips. The girl's dress was pulled up and she was being held down by an older woman.

We hauled the man off the girl and started questioning them all.

"Do you know these people?" I finally asked the little girl.

"They're . . . they're my grandma and grandpa," the girl stammered.

Engulfed by rage and nausea, my partner and I arrested all three and took them into the police station, where the two grandparents were booked and jailed. A female officer accompanied the little girl to a hospital so she could be examined, and then she was placed in child protective care.

A few weeks later, I was called to testify in the trial of the grandparents. I complied happily; I was eager to nail them. During my testimony, I was asked by the grandparents' hired attorney if I had actually seen the man's naked penis enter the girl's body. I said that when I had yanked him off her, both of their genitals had been naked, and I explained graphically what the guy had been doing when I grabbed him, convinced that my firsthand witness narrative would be enough to put him away.

The jury dismissed the case. The judge, whom I knew

personally, told me afterward that they did so because the hospital examination found no semen in the little girl, and I had not actually seen penetration, so there was no physical proof. *A few seconds later in the act, there would have been semen and possibly a pregnant little thirteen-year-old girl*, I thought angrily.

The couple was acquitted and the little girl released to other relatives in El Paso. I made an effort to purposely not plague myself with wondering about her future; there was nothing I could do, and it was too hard to think about.

Before I got onto car patrol, I had been on a walking beat, which is the usual breaking-in job for cops. I did a walking surveillance of my designated area, watching for suspicious activity, helping citizens in need, and making myself available for any person to beckon me for assistance with most anything.

One day while I was still on this beat, the manager of the largest and most beautiful theater downtown waved me over to come assist him at the ticket box. *The Saint Louis Blues* was being shown, with a cast of black musicians playing the popular music of the day.

When I approached, the manager pointed to three black soldiers in army uniform, standing in line to buy tickets. He told me to let them know he would not admit them, as it was a segregated theater.

It was 1957, and I knew this was the accepted procedure in many areas of the country at the time: businesses had the right to reject any customers without explanation, and racial exclusion in those days needed no explanation or justification. But as I approached the soldiers, all my brothers in arms in the navy flashed into my head, and I found this exclusion I was being directed to enforce repugnant and brutal. These were the same military men who'd fought for and protected every American's freedom and rights.

Still, I had a job to do, so, apologetically and sincerely, I explained the manager's decision, and the three men made a gentlemanly exit from the line.

When I saw the eruption of racial freedom marches in the 1960s, I thought it was surely about time.

As I was drifting out of my remembrances about police events while finishing my hair and shoe grooming, I resolved to resist the urge to share some of them with Ralph. I thought some of it was fun and entertaining, and he might enjoy hearing about it, but I didn't want to unduly encourage him to join the force—didn't want to risk him later feeling, if he didn't like police work, that I had pushed him into it.

I had craved travel since I was seven years old, had always loved being exposed to foreign cultures and bizarre people. I'd lapped up every minute of Mexico, China, Korea, Japan, Hawaii, and the numerous other lands I'd traveled to. I had no illusions about or strong expectations of people and didn't feel loneliness or anxiety in new venues but rather excitement and anticipation of all things new. My mom said I was a wild card. Through travel and cop work, I'd learned to adapt to anything. But Ralph was more of a stay-home guy. He was militarily disciplined and expected a certain standard of conduct from people, while I had abandoned such presumptions long ago.

I knew Ralph would have the same crazy experiences I'd had if he became a cop, but I would let him have the impact of surprise without forewarning, hoping he'd take to it with the same enthusiasm that had grabbed me.

CHAPTER 22

A Fist to the Face and One to the Gut

RALPH STRAIGHTENED WITH A jerk from his slouch of comfort on the sofa.

"God," he said in astonishment, peering through the front screen door, "here comes Anna, running like hell. And look, Mac's behind her."

I kicked open the screen door in time for Anna, my older cousin, to come racing through. She was obviously relieved to see my face at the doorway, knowing she'd reached safety.

Mac, her tattooed, prematurely bald, truck driver husband bolted up the stairs onto the porch, red-faced, and with obvious intentions of going through the same door after her. My fist slammed right into his nose, knocking him over the porch rail and onto the grass.

As Mac raised himself to his elbow, wiping the blood from his face, I strolled over to the rail. Evenly, with no contempt, almost patronizingly, I said, "Go on Mac, get your ass out of here."

Mac glared at me. I was eight years younger than him, and he had been a street fighter since he was four—but although I wasn't especially riled now, he knew any attempt to push things in this moment, especially with my cousin as a target, would really escalate the problem. I'm sure he remembered my begging him to arm wrestle when I was younger; then, he could put me down as the kid I was. But I wasn't a kid anymore.

Seeming to realize it wasn't worth the hassle, Mac wiped his bloody face and walked off with anger and bad intent in his eyes. He would settle with Anna later.

Ralph, watching at the open screen door, shifted to let me pass. I looked at Anna, knowing that her disposition, as fiery as my own, had probably helped her into this fix.

"Shit, Anna, why don't you get rid of that loser?" I asked half-heartedly, not expecting any real consideration of or response to my question.

Anna would get rid of him eventually. But right now, she popped open a beer and relaxed, happy to be in the security of her cousins' company.

Anna was beautiful and had a captivating personality. People liked to just listen to her talk, as she could never say anything calmly; everything was accentuated with full expression, and her outlook on life was light and humorous. Her high cheekbones and beautiful, flashing eyes were spellbinding—but she'd spellbound the wrong guy in Mac. He had no charm that I could find, just a lot of brawn and mouth, which had intrigued her somehow at first, but after a few months of being married to him and his loud barroom stories, she'd decided she couldn't stand him. Now she made her distaste plain by her every gesture—which, I was sure, was what had led to this latest uncontrolled attempt at her throat. Someday, I hoped, she would get rid of him.

"I got to get to work. Ralph, you are here for a while?" I asked.

Ralph nodded. He was mild-mannered, but I knew he wouldn't let anyone trespass on Anna and could hold his own if needed, so I relinquished the crisis to him and went down the front steps to await my ride to my shift.

Relaxed, I sucked the warm, dry air into my lungs and remembered the wet, sometimes suffocating air of the sea air during many of my naval tours. I detected a faint scent of beer from the corner bar. *Bunch of losers, boozing in the middle of the day*, I thought, picturing faceless people propped on a long row of stools. They always reminded me of a bunch of crows perched on a telephone wire. I'd never especially liked the smoky dark inside of a bar, although I got some occasional action there. I wasn't a daytime drinker.

I stood under the sole, scrawny tree in front of my dad's dilapidated house, waiting for my ride. My dad had never really given much effort to keeping the house up, although he did paint the trim haphazardly every few years. I guessed that with five unruly kids and their friends mutilating anything that was brought in, not to mention the pet dogs, cats, and chickens (I'd collected those as pets when I was young), he'd had to give up on any interior improvements to the house.

I grinned inside, remembering the swayback horse I had conned the milkman out of for a few bucks when I was eight. I'd brought it home and hid it in the back garage for a month, shoveling out dung and scrounging hay for it, riding it up and down the alley at night, until a neighbor reported me to the police. My mom had never even known it was there. I wondered now how she'd stood all the crap I had pulled. She'd always been fiercely proud of me, attributing what she called my charisma to her father, Lloyd. She was, I would think, the real inheritor of his charisma, as she was endlessly imaginative and amusing. My friends gravitated to her, and she was a gracious hostess to them all.

As I waited for my ride, I also reminisced about my dog Spotty—my childhood pet and constant companion, who I still missed.

One day during summer vacation when I was twelve years old, I left my dad's hot, run-down house pulling my wagon of cantaloupes to sell. I'd gotten them from a truck my dad had just brought in from Pecos, TX—another of his frequent trips to buy fruit for his fruit business on Overland Street. This was my first shot at making my own money so I could afford some better clothes and shoes, go to movies, and buy hamburgers.

I had only gone a couple of blocks and had sold a few melons when I heard a pitiful yelping coming from a little spotted black-and-white fox terrier that was lying in the street, struggling but not able to get up. I rushed over to lift it out of the way of oncoming cars, and its beautiful, kind, and helpless eyes looked straight at me in terror. It had been hit by a car and had a dangling, broken leg.

I put the dog on a big piece of cardboard that lay nearby, lifted her onto my wagon, and pulled her, atop the fruit, back to my house.

My sister, Tina, sixteen years old and very compassionate to animals, told me the dog's leg was broken for sure, and she helped me put a sling on its leg so she couldn't move it. We were not used to doctors, especially for a dog. We were used to doing things as best we could for ourselves, however, so we pulled the little leg into place and wrapped it. We petted the dog out of her state of shock, and she finally drank some water.

I immediately started calling my new dog Spotty. I petted and doctored her and placed her on a little cot on the back porch, where she lay for a couple days and had my constant attention.

I was amazed when, a few days later, Spotty got up and, hopping on three legs, unsteadily followed me into the kitchen. My mom told me to take the dog to a veterinarian a few blocks away since I was so stuck on her, so I did, but he wouldn't see her unless I had money. I only had two dollars, so I left, hoping my sling was going to work. About six weeks later, Spotty chewed the splint off. For the next few weeks, she got around with a small limp; after that, she healed completely and the limp disappeared.

She was my immediate sidekick, glued to my side. At night, she even got into bed with me and slept by my feet under the blankets. After four months, my mom got sick of having a dog around and told me to give her away, but I refused.

Spotty went to school with me and waited for me at the corner all day, until I returned to walk home with her. One day I came out of school and couldn't find her, so I hurried home, looking for her everywhere, afraid she'd been hit again. I burst into the house in a panic.

"Mom," I cried, "have you seen Spotty?"

"I took her on a bus and dropped her off in a stranger's yard," she said matter-of-factly. "I told you to get rid of that dog."

I was devastated. "Where did you take her?" I asked, desperate to find her.

My mom shook her head. "I already have a dog in the backyard, and your sister has that cat; that's enough. I'm having no more animals around."

I sure was in pain trying to go to sleep without my best little dog friend that night. The next day, though, at about six thirty in the evening, my dad and I heard a frantic scratching on the front screen door and I looked out to see Spotty's happy little begging face staring in at me.

My dad, who was really on my side in every situation, and I were both overjoyed and rushed to welcome Spotty home.

My mom gave up and said she could stay.

Spotty learned by herself to go up the school slide and then slide down. She also got on the merry-go-round by herself, holding on with her paws and having a great time. She was smarter than some of the people around my block.

One Friday afternoon, when I got to the grocery store by the school's corner where Spotty waited for me every day, the grocer told me a dog catcher had picked her up with a net. I was furious, and immediately started to think how I could get her back.

I knew where the dog pound was on Magoffin Street, and I went in a hurry. The guy there told me I had to pay for her shots, plus a ten-dollar fine, but I had no money and I knew I could not get it from home. "We've got seventy dogs in here," he said, "and they're all gonna be gassed in three days."

I could see Spotty in her cage, barking anxiously at me, but the guy wouldn't let me go near her.

I tried borrowing money from everyone but had no luck. Finally, I told my friend Johnny that they were going to kill my dog on Monday, and convinced him to help me get her out.

We went to the dog pound on Sunday afternoon, and after watching for a while, we saw the guard leave in a car with his wife. The pound was unguarded; it was our great luck and only chance.

The guard had locked the big gate to the pound, but Johnny and I climbed it. All the cages were made of chicken wire and were outdoors, with about ten dogs in each cage. I was prepared; I had wire cutters with me. I cut open Spotty's cage first, and with her ran out all the other dogs in the cage. They all squeezed through the iron fence and disappeared, so we cut open all the cages and released every dog. They all took off, yelping happily—except Spotty, who, of course, stayed by my side, barking her freedom call.

I grabbed Spotty and we took off running for home. For the next three weeks, I tied her up when I went to school so she wouldn't get out. My dad gave me fifty cents to take her to the fire department and get a rabies shot and tags so I wouldn't get fined if she ever got snagged by the dog catcher again.

A year later I got a job delivering newspapers, so, since Spotty had gone with me to sell melons and do everything else, she did the paper route with me. She watched me fling papers onto porches for a couple days, and then I let her try: I put one in her mouth. Right away, she ran the paper up and dropped it on the porch. She was incredibly smart! It seemed like she'd thought of it herself.

One rainy morning, Spotty and I were sitting inside a stairway to an apartment house on Montana Street for shelter when we heard a loud argument from the apartment next to us, and then a gunshot. Spotty perked her ears and cocked her head sideways, like, "What was that?"

We both quietly and quickly ran out of there.

That afternoon, as I delivered the evening paper, the *El Paso Herald Post* headlines were, "Woman Kills Husband on Montana Street."

I kept delivering papers there, but I never sat in that place for shelter again.

Spotty and I made our paper rounds for a year and a half. She was always up and ready to go at the right time every morning, and she knew when the evening start time was, too. She ran and worked tirelessly. I don't know if I have ever been that close to a person in my life. She learned every trick a dog could do, and some new ones, too. She even explored caves with me on Mt. Franklin's eastern slopes, all the way to the top.

As I grew into my teen years, my feeling of closeness to Spotty faded a little as my world spread out to motorcycle trips to Ruidoso with Paul and working in a downtown movie theater. I was always adventurous and always needed money, and Spotty couldn't always go with me to the places I was going. She stayed home with my dad and began to follow him—kind of in a lonely way, he would tell me. I always loved her, and she never lost her uncontrolled joy at seeing me come home, but I'm sure she missed our jobs and fun. We sure didn't hit the merry-go-round anymore.

After I came back to El Paso and joined the police department following my four years of wildly exciting travel and mind-impressing experiences and sights, I was always happy to see my little aging friend when I visited my dad (she stayed with my dad due to my erratic life and hours). To rub her ears and pet her as she settled so lovingly onto my lap was always a fond reminder of my undiminished, warm connection with her.

One ominous day, after a tiring shift at work, I stopped by my dad's house to see him and Spotty and he told me heavily and apologetically, looking sadly into my eyes, that the maid had taken Spotty to the store with her and Spotty had gotten hit by a car, for the second time in her life, and it had this time killed her. The stab of pain was severe, despite all the death I had seen as a policeman, and kept its place as a primary, serious grief—the loss of a lifetime friend. It was a fist to the gut.

I still hold Spotty dear to my heart.

CHAPTER 23

Now A Detective

I STOOD ON THE sidewalk, waiting for my ride to work to arrive. I had now been on the PD for three and a half years, and I wanted to move up to detective. I was friends with some guys who were agitating to pull me in, so I waited hopefully for the promotion.

I broke into a grin of fond recognition as Glen pulled to the curb. Glen had been promoted to the "Dicks"—Detectives division—eight months earlier, and was one of the people pulling for me to get in. I was on good terms with the captain and my chances, I knew, were good. I was a little tired of the uniform.

"The chief wants to see you soon as you get in, David," Glen announced as I got into his car, which far outpriced a car most detectives could afford. "I'll bet you're in."

"Let's go see," I said simply. Making detective was the transfer most sought after uniformed patrol work, since it offered more intriguing work, investigating and solving criminal activity. After three years on car patrol, I wanted to move up in the department or get out.

I had answered a distress call in the tenements the night before and found a woman having a baby with no time to get to a hospital. Her young daughter screamed for me to do something, compelling me to stand close and try to catch the coming baby; it came with a twin, and her water broke all over my shirt and arms as the two made their entrance into the world. I helped escort the two slippery babies into life. Only when emergency help finally arrived was I free to go home and throw up. It was the second birthing I'd been slammed into during my tenure as a policeman, and I wanted no more! I was a little mad at the ignorance of the woman for lying there until the last minute before calling the police to deliver her babies. I never wanted to get pressed into that again.

Detective division would remove me from those unpleasant situations. More money, more prestige, plain clothes, more authority, more leeway to work my own angles—my enthusiasm was pleasantly mounting.

"Yeah, let's go see," I repeated.

Glen was right. I was surprised how swiftly I was moved in. I started that day. The chief shook my hand warmly, gave me the news unceremoniously, and left it to Glen to introduce me to the other Dicks, whom I already knew on a first-name basis. They were all pleased with my appointment. I was a regular guy like them all and fit in easily.

I started in Narcotics and Bunco. This was precisely up my alley. I'd lived around this activity all my life, so investigating it wouldn't be that hard. I didn't have to build up contacts or stoolies. Most of the kids I grew up with were on the street. The PD had just put me in my own pond to swim, and I knew every lily pad.

"C'mon, let's drop by my dad's house so I can shed this uniform," I said, grinning at Glen, after the chief gave me my promotion. I was excited with my new situation and wanted to tell my family.

"Damn, I'm glad you're in," laughed Glen.

My mom and sister were home to receive the news. They talked nonstop and excitedly when I told them. Glen sat on the dilapidated sofa, waiting for his new partner to get into his civilian clothes and eyeing Anna.

I liked Glen, but he used and discarded women—whom he attracted with very little effort—like Kleenex. He exerted no effort to keep them around, because he didn't care if they stayed. He was not strikingly handsome, but his tallness, self-assuredness, smoothness, and quiet moodiness exuded a definite strong pull on women. They all wanted to be the one to reform him; he let them try, and while they were trying, he got what he wanted. By the time they even suspected the futility of their effort, he had been saturated with their favors and was ready to cut them loose, so their indignation during their parting was always of little interest to Glen.

He had grown up an only child, and his mother married one well-off man after another, totaling six "daddies" for Glen by the time he reached twenty-two years old. She had indulged him and shared her good financial fortune with him, always giving him enough cash that he was able to live a lifestyle well above what a detective's income allowed. He used his money and suave manner to impress women.

He was eyeing Anna, but he would not make a move on my family. He also knew that Anna would be a match for him. She was wise, smart, and cocky—an actual challenge.

As my cousin, she was out of his range anyway.

I was anxious to begin my new job. I immediately sensed the lower-key atmosphere as I blended in easily and quickly in the "Dicks Division," and I liked it; it was nice to be in an office with amicable associates, without the stress of interacting with irate, conflicted, unbalanced, drunk, bizarre, or dangerous street criminals. Thieves, house invaders, wife beaters, and gang rovers looking for action were the street norm, and in order to subdue an offender, a street cop or cycle cop often had to engage in sudden and extreme physical interaction, which often escalated into actual combat.

The adrenaline-pumping action of my former cop assignments was now replaced with conversational interaction with persons, whether as suspects, witnesses, or victims of reported crimes. It was important and had a compelling level of interest and mystery, but the amount of cases put on my desk to investigate and solve—five or six daily, with no database or computer search engines to assist in moving the case toward conclusion—was overwhelming. The load seemed insurmountable and thus, for the most part, unsolvable. Detectives were forced by demand to just move daily cases on to a next-day status for attention, which meant that many cases didn't remain active targets of attention for long. Simply put: too much criminal activity and too little time to deal with it, even with overtime.

I applied myself dutifully, and initially with peak interest, to my detective work, but eventually my interest waned, since I couldn't pursue substantiation of my case leads. The job was comfortable, but comfort had never been my turf, and I found myself missing the street's challenges; I even missed the emotionally disturbing upheaval that I had longed to escape.

I began considering, after a year of probing into petty and grand crime situations as a Dick, using the police and investigative acumen I had acquired to do my own crime solving and investigating for private clients. I partnered with another guy and opened a small office as a private investigator, and found immediate interest in the service. With that, I made a final, irreversible decision to leave the police department and fully commit to opening my own detective business.

Just as all this was happening, I saw a young woman at a grand hotel ballroom dance who purposely, while pretending to be unaware of my being seated in her path, passed by my table. She immediately became the center of my focus, as I swiftly recognized her as the girl to whose home I'd been called twice: first when she was just seventeen and had been robbed at a grocery store, and then to investigate a Peeping Tom at her bathroom window when she was nineteen. She would now be twenty-two, and, seeing that she had reached her full beauty and an approachable age, I resolved I would not let her vanish again.

I had a date with me, so I sent a friend to join her group and invite her and her date to a holiday party I planned to attend two nights later; there, I would be free to pursue my fascination with her.

Part IV: David and Patricia

CHAPTER 24

Life and Love Tsunami

Patricia

God it was all fun! It was the Christmas holiday season, and I was at a dance at the elegant Hilton Hotel, which had a wooden dance floor and orchestra, when I saw a strikingly handsome guy seated with a girl and another couple at the end of a table next to the dance floor. I was wearing an exquisite, off-the-shoulder, blue chiffon, form-fitting dress and felt the best path to the dance floor, when my date asked me to dance, was one that would take me past this guy. I was told later that as I passed by his chair, he took a fork and gently lifted the back hem of my dress—all in playful jest, but he was for sure interested. I also learned later that he had sent a friend, who happened to know my date, to approach our table of friends and invite us to a small house party a couple nights later. We went.

David

I was comfortably seated on the floor, leaning against the wall with a drink in my hand and a girl by my side. We were at a small house party. New Year's Eve, bringing in 1962, was a day away, and I—now twenty-seven years old—sat complacently, musing about my erratic life of world exploration, travels, and adventures, expecting or needing nothing dynamic to occur. The casual party in a small apartment promised no adventure or finale.

And then the door opened.

I threw a casual glance in that direction—and what was coming through the door held my eyes and increased my attention. It was her again: the girl I had manipulated to be invited with her date to this party. This time I wasn't going to miss her. Since I'd last seen her at nineteen, she had exceeded the beauty I had remembered and developed into an enticingly voluptuous woman. She had a nonassertive demeanor; she was elegantly beautiful. I waited a bit, but as she put a cigarette to her lips, I stepped over to her, offered a light, and said to her, "We have met before."

"We have?" she responded softly, and with interest. "When was that?"

I lit her cigarette. "Remember when you had the Peeping Tom?"

She looked shaken and a bit put off as she stepped back and responded, "That was you?"

I looked commandingly into her irresistible green eyes and secured my hit with, "No, I was the cop who answered the call."

It was on. We were married four months later.

Happy days

Loving life

Patricia

I noticed him as I walked into the door of the party with my date. He was broad-shouldered, with a square jaw, thick head of hair, muscular build, hazel eyes, and an unmistaken, natural, and easy all-male essence that exuded a compelling and captivating presence. His laugh was strong and revealed perfect white teeth. I didn't stare, as my mind had snapped his picture two days earlier. He was the same guy I had purposely passed by going to the dance floor at the Hilton Hotel.

After a while, he casually stepped away from his date and walked up to me to light my cigarette and told me we had met before. I did not recognize him as the good-looking cop who had come to my home when I was nineteen because some guy, a Peeping Tom, had been hanging off my dad's roof in the dark, staring at me through the bathroom window, as I showered. Neither did I remember his first visit when I was seventeen and was robbed at a grocery store by a poor kid pretending to have a gun.

I remembered now that the officer who'd responded to the Peeping Tom call had talked to me in the living room and told my dad to look around the back for any dropping of evidence so he could talk to me further. We had stepped out onto the front sidewalk and had a few minutes of conversation, during which our mutual attraction under the moonlight had been palpable.

When this handsome stranger told me he was the cop who had answered both calls, I was sure I wouldn't forget this third meeting at the small, casual party to which he had quietly arranged for my date and I to be invited.

He made sure that for the next week, during the Christmas and New Year's holidays, I would be where he was. That night, he asked my date and me to join his date and him with a few other people who were leaving the party to go to a New Mexico nightclub for a few drinks and music. I could see my date wanted no part of it, but I did, so we drove to the club and met up with the others.

The dance music was good at the club and soon David, that good looking ex-cop, told one of his friends to ask his date to dance so he would be free to ask me.. When we got to the floor, I was thinking, *He's so handsome and manly, if he just doesn't say something groveling or stupid . . .* And he sure didn't. His conversation and dance moves were mildly flirtatious, but not fawning or overly solicitous. We had one dance and the glue took. The next night was New Year's Eve, so he again invited my date and me to go to a New Year's party at his friend's house.

My date and I arrived at a small New Year's Eve party at the home of David's friend, where he was also in attendance with his same previous date. I was wearing my black and oh-so-form-fitting, low-cut New Year's Eve dress.

David didn't goggle or interact with me that night, but I was sure I had him. We all had a bit to drink and I noticed he was never inebriated and always in control, with a flashing laugh and strong but not pushy presence.

When midnight hit and the cheering and celebrating came, I went to the restroom to wait it out, as I knew the men rushing to grab kisses was going to happen and I always ducked that. When I came out after the noise subsided, David came over to me for the first time in the evening and asked me to dance. He asked me where I had disappeared to and I told him where and why I had made myself unavailable.

"So," I said innocently, "I haven't been kissed."

He leaned down as we swayed to a dance, so very masculine, but gently, and gave me a kiss. It was a very good kiss—respectful, but sexy and commanding. It was the kiss that was perfectly measured. This guy knew what he was doing and was in every way in control; he showed no weakness or lack of surety in any area.

With that, David assumed his place at the top of my list. After New Year's, we were together every night and day, caught in a furor of quick attachment and entrancement.

Nightclubbing in Juarez, partying with friends, and cozy evenings getting entrapped in each other's hearts and habits was my and David's new agenda. I was in my last year of college, and I had plenty of "date David" time. He picked me up daily at the Queen of Angels Catholic boarding establishment I had moved to in order to be closer to the college I attended.

At the boarding house, I had my own room and bath. Available to share with the numerous other boarders was a common dining area and large living and reception area downstairs. Only females were allowed to live there, but males could enter the reception area to pick up their female relatives or dates. The house was run by nuns who allowed the girls there (many were working girls; I was the only college student) to sunbathe in the small enclosed courtyard, but only if they did so in a modest dress, as shorts or bathing suits were not allowed. The doors were locked at midnight every evening and would not be opened to latecomers, so I often spent a late night at my parents' house.

David often took me to the old Hacienda Restaurant, one of the oldest and most elaborate homes of a settling family two hundred years earlier, on our dates. It was a historical site: Don Juan de Onate had led a Spanish expedition through that spot in 1508 in discovering the Pass to the North, and in 1849, Simeon Hart had built Hart's Mill and elaborate private residence on the edge of the Rio Grande River, which marks the border between Texas and Mexico, there as well. Between 1873 and 1893, the officers' quarters of the Original Fort Bliss were erected close by. The elegant residence became a restaurant in 1940, and by the time David and I were dating was a sought-out dining establishment, known for its rustic furnishings exemplifying early Southwest history and embellished with ample photos of the original family occupants, whose fireplace, bedrooms, elegant dining areas, elaborate courtyards, and even their outside horse tethers for early-incoming riders, were still standing. The walls also still bore the original painted family portraits of those who had lived there, wearing their long-since outdated apparel of the times, giving customers a sense of living in the historic past.

There were a few places in New Mexico to go to dance, eat, and drink, like the King's X, which we sometimes occasioned, but Juarez, with its ample party and dining atmosphere, was our usual date destination. In those days ladies often wore cocktail dresses to the more elegant clubs, so the evenings were special. We danced to orchestra music at the Charmont or to rock music by Long John at the Lobby, which hosted a constant flow of high-spirited nightclub-goers, some heavily clustered around the circular, open bar, others dancing to the blaring music on a crowded floor of gyrating bodies. It was a carnival-like atmosphere. Between us, David and I had quite a network of friends, which gave us a busy social life.

In the later part of our first four months together, David took my hand as we sat in a booth at a downtown Oasis next to the Plaza Theater, slipped a diamond ring onto my left-hand ring finger, and said, "Don't take it off."

I didn't want to assume it was an engagement ring, because he hadn't mentioned marriage, so I just said, "It's beautiful. What is it?"

I didn't want to be embarrassed if he meant it as some kind of friendship ring.

He said simply, "An engagement ring."

The sealer words! We didn't make a date or a plan. But a month later, we went to Juárez in the afternoon to eat and were having a pleasant warm afternoon together when David said, "Let's get married."

I thought it was a delicious idea. I didn't even think it odd for me to be wearing my form-fitting black lace dress. He took me to some city office, and we were married by a justice of the peace in Mexican legalese. Then we went to the beautiful Charmont Club and sat at the round bar, which had a piano situated in the bar's interior floor, as the pianist played classical music for which he was known and which I had always loved to hear.

We were both very excited and thrilled at our spontaneous plunge into being a married couple. David got a bar phone, called his mother, and told her we had married. We had a celebratory drink, and then headed back to my parents' house in El Paso.

Wedding night—instant love that couldn't wait

We arrived in the very early evening. We went into the house and I hung the Mexican marriage certificate on the door for my parents to see. They weren't too surprised, and I thought it was such a great announcement. David called his parents and they both came over to meet my parents and have a celebratory drink. It was that simple, and that magnificent.

After finding out how David and I had been married, some of my relatives and friends began to agitate that I should be married a second time, this time in a church—a traditional wedding. I was not enthusiastic, as I was not by nature very ceremonious and wondered how two marriages would make me more happy than the one I was living in. At the nudging of these family members and friends, though, I began to inquire at a local parish.

The husband, the dad

Tsunami time

The parish priest told me that if we wanted to be married there, certain documents were required of David to validate that he was a baptized Catholic. David's baptism had taken place in Mexico when he lived there with his uncles for two years as a young boy, so he wrote to his Mexican relatives and asked that they go to the cathedral in Mexico City where he'd been baptized to secure his baptismal certificate. They did, and sent it to us in El Paso; when it arrived, I turned it in to the parish priest, fulfilling the suggestions of friends but not an important desire of my own, as marrying a second time felt redundant. And besides, in the brief time we'd been married, we'd created a busy schedule for ourselves; who had the time for all this?

The issue dissolved when I got a call from the parish explaining that the priest in charge of my upcoming marriage had left the church with his lover, and none of the documents could be found. No extensive plans had been arranged, so we abandoned the idea altogether. I was relieved that we could now get back to the essence of our new life. It turned out that one marriage was just right for me. We surged into our future.

On my Juárez wedding night, my dad prepaid our night at the Caballero Motel close by, where we often went to swim. The motel housed us for the few nights it took for David to rent us our own apartment on Stanton Street. My new husband gave me money to shop for essential dishes and household needs, and that began our dynamic journey of life as a married couple.

CHAPTER 25

Inescapable Descent into Racism

Patricia

I made the decision to quit college, although I had only nine college credits left to complete and one semester of student teaching left to do, and despite the fact that David did not think it was a good idea. I did it because I knew I had enough college courses to be hired as a social worker with the Texas Department of Public Welfare (a good friend who was a state welfare worker had told me how interesting the job was).

I was a quick hire and soon David drove me to Tyler, TX, to do a month-long training course. It was a serious eye opener to a culture I had never experienced. The prejudice was all-consuming. It was the early 1960s, and there were signs everywhere in front of public places and stores that said "Mexicans not Allowed" and "Blacks not Allowed." Because my name was now Rodriguez, people often asked me if I was white, which I so conspicuously was.

In our daily classes, we sat in groups of about twenty to be informed of requirements and procedures for people to apply for and receive welfare. My area of interest was aid to dependent children, who were usually being raised without a father. At one point a woman instructor asked the class, as she was instructing us in procedures used to communicate with the welfare recipients, how a black male should be addressed, and she called on me to answer.

"What's his age?" I asked. I didn't understand the question.

"It doesn't matter," the instructor said. "A black male of any age."

I was sincerely perplexed. "If he was over eighteen, I would address him as 'Mister' and his surname."

The group's disapproval was made apparent by their expressions and even a gasp or two.

"It is obvious Mrs. Rodriguez, not being familiar with our culture, does not know that the proper and only acceptable way to address a black man is by his first name," our instructor said loudly. "He is never referred to as 'Mister.'"

She went on to explain that Mr. automatically indicates the man is white. I was also informed that black women were not "Mrs." but just called by their first name. I was stunned.

At break time, as I stood outside the classroom door, a young white man glanced at me and commented within my hearing range, "If I ever heard a white woman call a black man 'Mr.,' I'd slap her in the face."

That really put the fright into me. I realized this culture was seriously steeped in southern Christianity and racial prejudice without noticing the conflict between the two.

After we'd been trained in the basics, all of us new employees were sent out into the surrounding country areas, alone, to interview welfare recipients or applicants. I had David's car—he had left it with me after he drove me to Tyler and taken a bus back to El Paso—so I was able to drive myself to the dwellings of the welfare applicants and recipients. The neighborhoods were shabby and unsafe looking.

I could not feel comfortable calling a grown man or woman by their first name, so when I went to the addresses on my list, I asked for Mrs. Mary Wilkins or Mr. Joe Wilkins—but each time, the black responders said there was no one in the area by that name.

After a few times of not finding the person at the address I was given, one of the black women said, "Do you know you're asking for white folk when you say Mr. or Mrs.?"

I then knew to comply, but I did so grudgingly, as I was participating in a discriminatory practice.

Finally, I completed my month of training, and my handsome husband rode the bus back up to get me. It was like a honeymoon: we went to Six Flags Over Texas and rode the Ferris wheel and roller coaster. It was joyous to be with him and on my way back to my family, from which I had never really been separated before.

I told David about the prejudice and he said, totally unruffled, that he'd seen it all his life. He was really an adaptor, totally unconcerned by others' issues or hang-ups. He always had this life-maneuvering agility. It served him well.

I was with the Welfare Department six months and found the whole scope of involvement in the clients' lives and needs overwhelming. This was a downtrodden element of the population I had never before encountered. The job also demanded longer working hours and days than a teacher put in, and for much less pay and benefits. I began to see I had jumped away from a good occupation to a very demanding and fruitless job.

After six months, I rushed to get back into college and finish the degree in elementary education in which I had already invested three and a half years; I wanted to return to what I had loved and now missed.

I got that degree and became a teacher—a job I loved for twenty-five years. The hours were compatible with my kids' own school hours, and I had all holidays off, and the summer too. It required a great leap to catch the boat I had nearly let depart from shore without me, but I'm still grateful that I jumped when I did.

CHAPTER 26

Being A Private Eye

David

I'd left the force knowing that as a private investigator, I could use my long history of experience with snitches, snoops, criminals, and of confidentially collecting information from or about others for work, to my advantage. It was my racetrack already; I just transferred it over to the business side. I partnered with a guy of similar background.

My earliest case involved a woman whose two young kids had been snatched from her and whisked away to another city a month earlier by her ex-husband. She was in frantic distress. She had legal full custody of the kids and a new, rich husband who had a private plane, which meant she could afford to track them fast. Her new husband knew the ex-husband worked as a car dealership manager in Houston, so he flew her, my partner, and me to Houston in his four-seat airplane. An attorney had recommended us for the job of retrieving her kids.

In Houston, I scouted the schools in the area of the ex's house, then we rented a car and all went to his dealership.

There, from a safe distance, the wife pointed out her ex-husband to me. I have a strong memory and can quickly imprint a face in my memory without long study, so after a few seconds, I knew my lead man.

We rented two rooms in a motel near the dealership, and my partner and I returned to the dealership to stake the ex out until he left work, at which time we followed him at a discreet distance to his home. We reported back to the husband and wife, saying that since it was Saturday, an opportunity to grab the kids was unlikely to present itself; they probably would not be separated from the dad or leave his house. I suggested we wait until Monday and find out if he took them to a school, where our access would be greater.

The husband had urgent business to do in El Paso, as did my partner, so the two of them left me and the wife alone, saying they trusted us to make the kids' retrieval happen.

"Once you have the kids," the husband said, "call me, and it will take me only five hours to fly down and pick you all up."

Monday, the wife and I staked out the house early in the morning, but only the husband came out; a full day and evening of surveillance gave us no sighting of the children.

The mother was exhausted and emotionally seared, so the next day, I left her to rest in the motel and did the surveillance alone. I saw nothing Tuesday. Finally, when I returned Wednesday, I saw a daycare van arrive at 9:00 a.m. and watched the two boys, ages three and five, leave the front door, escorted by the husband's new wife, and climb into the van. I followed the bus as it weaved down a few streets, picking up other kids, and finally stopped at a daycare center, then sped back to the motel, where I reported back to the mother and told her we would race to the private airport as soon as we got the kids.

She had a statement that she had written herself, declaring that she was the mother of the children. As we waited outside the daycare at 12:00 p.m., the children filed out into a play area with a daycare worker. I stayed behind the wheel as the mother quickly jetted out of the car and at a rapid pace, crossed the street into the play area, and brusquely handed the letter to the worker. When the children saw her, they ran to her, and she grabbed their wrists and raced back to my car.

"Lie down on the floor!" I commanded as I drove off; I could see the daycare woman running out after them, trying, futilely, to catch us.

"Bring those kids back now!" the woman screeched. "I'm calling the police."

I had smeared my license plates with mud for protection, and I kept my face hidden as we sped off to the private airport, outside the city limits, to meet the plane, which was scheduled to land any minute.

As she ran back into the building, I could already hear sirens closing in on us. Amazingly, one of the cop cars passed by and looked right at me, but I inconspicuously and nonchalantly glanced back and kept driving, and they didn't pull me over.

We were on the plane and outward bound within the hour. The job was done and the pay was more than generous, reflecting the mother's gratitude and relief.

As a fourth-year college student, Patricia was totally enthusiastic to have me enroll in university again and complete the studies I'd begun sporadically as a cop. In my earlier years on the force I had enrolled in college, but the grueling night shifts and lack of sleep, coupled with having day duty as well, had totally disrupted my class schedule and forced me to drop the pursuit of attending university on a regular basis. I had dropped out very regretfully, however, so I was happy that I now had an opportunity to go for it again. My gnawing intention of one day being able to resume the pursuit of the formal education that my worldly travels and adventures had interrupted was now on my agenda again.

After Patricia graduated from university, I was hired as a campus cop at her alma mater, and simultaneously relinquished my holding in my PI agency. Patricia was now an accredited elementary teacher. She'd completed her degree at Texas Western College (since renamed The University of Texas at El Paso, and so named when I enrolled). Unfortunately, because she was three months pregnant with our first child when she completed her education, she could not be hired by the public school system; at that time, a woman could not teach past her first trimester of pregnancy.

Since public school was out, she got a job teaching third grade at St. Pius Catholic School following her conclusion of university classes.

Patricia

Catholic School was an easy place to get a teaching job. The pay was low because few teachers had a degree in teaching and most weren't certified. Working at St. Pius was an opportunity for me to get a few months' income before the school year ended and I birthed our first baby.

I had gone to a Catholic school in St. Louis, so I knew

the heavily dogmatic religious curriculum, which required forty minutes a day of religious instruction—time sapped from the instruction of history and science. Not just behavior but also thought was stifled and controlled at the school. But it was very smooth sailing, at least: the parents were cooperative and non-confrontational.

Each day at St. Pius began with a religious ceremony, mass, that all children and staff attended in church. Hourly prayers were said by the entire class, as were before-lunch, after-lunch, and end-of-the-school-day prayers.

Discipline problems were rare. Uniforms were required. Students were taken weekly to confess their sins to a priest in a confessional and receive forgiveness. I was relieved that I had completed my college degree and was a certified teacher. It was my ticket to one day return to the undisciplined and harried, but also open-thinking, market of public education.

David

Patricia delivered our first child in July of the following summer. She began teaching in the El Paso Independent School District a year and a half later, and was assigned to a school in a lower-socioeconomic and crime-abundant area I had patrolled as a policeman. We moved into an apartment on campus with our eighteen-month-old daughter, Patrice.

During this time, my wife was my primary motivator, giving me the love, encouragement, and unrelenting commitment I needed in order to take up my formerly interrupted academic pursuit and go after it again. She was unwavering. I could finally get enough rest at night, being free of rotating shift work, and with Patricia's support was able to establish an uninterrupted work and study schedule. She went to teach school daily, and we had a maid care for our little girl and clean the house.

I often picked up my daughter after work and took her with me to campus. I would take her to Kidd Field to watch the football team practice—an outing she loved—or to eat with my friends at a cafeteria off campus. If a jukebox were playing, she would dance with enthusiasm to the music.

Patrice often played with other little kids outside our apartment. One day I commented in front of them that I had to get my car washed, because it was looking dirty. I stepped into the apartment door to get a juice drink as the kids continued playing, and when I came back outside, they were all using their tongues to lick the dirt off the fenders. I had to wash off all their tongues. I was learning fatherhood.

Despite our busy schedules, we still had ample time to visit our families, and we had a large circle of friends with whom we spent weekends socializing at backyard barbecues with our kids. We often got a babysitter in the evenings so we could continue to soak up the dinner, dancing, and fun goings-on in Juarez, where we still went often, keeping our life injected with a lot of fun.

It was on campus that I met Dr. Ellenton, the professor who eventually led me to the mines in Mexico.

I also developed personal friendships with several university professors in the fields of economics, history, and especially sociology. Over the course of many impromptu conversations, we explored the historic and economic origins of the multicultural and heavily prejudiced Mexican and American populations. The time I'd spent as a detective in the criminal area of narcotics and bunco, rampant in both cultures, gave me many insights not available in textbooks.

A reciprocal exchange of interest and information evolved between me and these professors, as my own world travel and extensive experiences with multiple cultures in the US, Asia, and Mexico gave us common conversational grounds. Their academic interpretations of population demographics, including in the areas of prejudice, economics, and history, held compelling interest to me.

My education was not singularly academic. I became an insurance salesman during this time; the many students who were moderately interested in having insurance coverage but who defaulted on policy payments made commissions sporadic and fluctuating, however.

I next became involved with friends of mine whose occupation was real estate. Impressed with their financial gains, I gradually veered in this direction. My interest, over the university years, eased away from philosophical and political conversations with the faculty guys to the hard-dollar economic perspectives of the commercial real estate guys.

My wife was secure and even passionate in her teaching job, so we were on a solid financial footing. My career interests careened fast and permanently toward commercial real estate.

Patricia

As a social worker, I had visited and serviced welfare clients categorized as Aid to the Blind, Old Age Assistance, and Aid to Totally and Permanently Disabled, but I had primarily worked with dependent children—my preferred group to assist, and to which I had asked to be assigned. The children I worked with were of Mexican descent, all poverty stricken and from one-parent families (always a single mother), and ranging in age from newborns to sixteen years of age. Some families consisted of up to eight or more children.

These families resided in heavily populated areas, all being of similar demographics, which were: no income, uneducated and unemployed young unwed mothers, single or divorced middle-aged mothers, and many illegal immigrants with American-born children. They all were dependent on welfare, food stamps, and free school lunch programs. The only healthcare they had access to was limited, government-provided healthcare—or, if that could not be acquired, the frequent use of a local hospital, which by law could not refuse emergency room patients. Hospitals in El Paso consequently had an overload of poor mothers bringing their children to the emergency rooms for simple ailments, as that was an assured, and often their only, resource for medical care.

One of the most destitute, expansive housing areas I visited my clients in, composed of two and three levels of apartments over several blocks, was so filthy and disintegrated that it was known as "The Seven Hells" and harbored danger for both its residents and the welfare workers and police who visited it. It was drug ridden, and full of aggressive, bullying gangs engaged in constant struggles for control of their "turf"—which was actually publicly financed and owned streets, neighborhood dwellings, and commercial zones. Children who ventured down to the sidewalks alone were in danger of encountering sexual predators, who also hovered around the only common bathroom provided in each apartment for all the tenants to share. Those bathrooms also served as refuges for drug sales, exchanges, and consumption.

The halls in these buildings were dark and cluttered with trash. When a woman opened her door to my knock, she would typically be submissive, emotionally drawn down, overwrought, and surrounded with children in a tiny, crowded room with only a single bed for the whole family. Most children in these apartments, I knew, slept on a floor with a scant blanket for warmth. Boxes often served as cribs for newborn babies.

Some of these women did have men or divorced husbands living with them—but always unofficially, as their known presence would endanger the women's right to collect her welfare check.

When my work brought me to the most threatening areas, I had my husband accompany me for safety. I was always uneasy as I made my visits into these cavernous neighborhoods, but was also shocked and unnerved by this exposure to an America my college classes in sociology, history, civics, and economics, and my overall years of required readings and lectures, had never given me an insight into. Seeing this population and their desperate struggles made my jaw drop. The stunning and deeply ingrained awareness these experiences gave me became integrated into my social and political database of information, which allowed me to more empathetically assess and interpret population needs and economic spending proposals city and nationwide. I was grateful for this exposure to the underlying misery and poverty I now knew existed in the entire country.

I took this new perspective with me as I chose to teach elementary school in these same barrio areas. I felt I had a deep understanding of my students' culture and needs. This was a career and population I loved, and it felt like a mission I could not abandon.

CHAPTER 27

The Finishing Line, The Starting Line

David

After four years, I put on the graduation gown and walked up to the podium to receive a handshake and my degree. I was thirty-two years old. My wife, my dad (Jefe), and my friends sat in the football stadium audience. My dad, I'm told, said as I reached out to accept my diploma, "His mother would be so proud if she had lived to see this."

My passion for travel still alive, the turmoil and apprehension of my police department years behind me, the enticement and potential of commercial real estate waiting, and the warm fulfillment of being a dad and husband all around me—all this rolled into a fast-forward cannonball of intense motivation.

The seeking and wonderment of my youth had faded, but the adventurism and energy had not subsided—it had just been reincorporated into a thrust for financial success and stability, and real estate was now my fishing grounds. Those years of living in and often visiting Mexico had established in me not only a fluency in the language but also an understanding of the lifestyles, values, and socially expected and accepted mannerisms of Mexican culture; I was well equipped to receive the trust and respect given by my father's people to one who belonged. This had been exactly the purpose of my father's gift of sending me to Mexico. Now, having the know-how to do business among wealthy people from Mexico was like carrying a big wad of cash in my pocket: it really bought my way into their trust and acceptance. I was ready to deal.

I knew where the fish were but I needed the bait: a real estate license. I needed to attend real estate classes, study every angle of the business, both residential and commercial, and pass the test to become a certified agent. I needed time to study all this, clearly, but also needed immediate income to move us out of the university family housing we were leaving and rent a house, so I took a job with the El Paso school system as an elementary coach; this gave me the income I needed to help support our family, and I used every break time to study for the real estate exam. I was motivated to get into an area that could serve up big money and was completely resolved not to give another year to coaching, which was mundane and offered abysmal pay.

At the school year's end, I took the test and got my real estate license. It was a humble beginning, but that's where I had always started: at the bottom, looking up. I knew there was a huge amount still to learn but I saw the good profit a friend who I had grown up with and who had established his own real estate business was bringing in, so I went to work with him. The pressure was on to make it. I had a family to support.

A lucrative field was selling houses to low-income people who qualified for a US government–guaranteed loan that was designed to allow a population with bad credit ratings to qualify for housing. This group of home seekers was eager to buy, and I was eager to make rapid and plentiful sales while the program was in effect.

The commissions I made from these sales bought our first home on Tyrone Street in a beautiful, safe, eastside community, and when we brought our second-born girl, Tresha, home, we were able to put her into her ready baby bed, in her own bedroom, with a ready rocking chair. Patrice, by then five years old, put her feet on the lower rail of the baby bed and lifted herself high enough to stare down at her new sister. Enraptured, she showered her with a love that never diminished.

Soon, I began to expand my interest into the more profitable side of my new business: commercial real estate. I started attending seminars in El Paso, Las Vegas, Phoenix, Dallas, and Houston, determined to hear from the best available presenters in the field. Over a few years, I attended fifteen commercial sales and exchange seminars. The informational output was massive—a lot to digest and master—but was also a more compact and extensive education than university courses ever offered me, and one promising a much more lucrative monetary future. I had to go this way, as that's where the money was.

There was more to master in selling commercial, so sales weren't as frequent as they had been when I'd sold houses, but one sale gave a handsome commission, as the dollars being dealt were big. I sought out and met wealthy investors, several of which were from Mexico. They felt very comfortable with me, as I thoroughly understood their language and culture. I would become friends with them and their families and socialize with them outside of an office setting—dining and traveling with them to acquaint them with areas outside of El Paso like Ruidoso, New Mexico, and Las Vegas.

My Mexican customers usually spoke competent but not extensive English, and their wives' and children's English skills were nonexistent or limited, so they appreciated the security of my being their spokesman in travel or business. Mexicans are family centered; true hospitality, especially in the 1960s, '70s, and '80s, meant inviting them to your home. So I invited them, knowing that was a move superior to just treating them to dinner at any fine restaurant. Because of this, these clients became lifelong friends and felt as secure with me as if they were doing business in Mexico (and a lot *more* secure as far as the legality of the transactions was concerned).

Early on, I met a Mexican from Torreon who exactly fit that description: he was a wealthy cattle owner with his own extensive ranch who brought herds of cattle to El Paso to sell. When I met him we became good friends, and his trust in me as a fellow Mexican prompted him to inquire about investment possibilities for him in El Paso. I took him around and introduced him to property owners; I traveled with him to Las Vegas, where he liked to gamble alongside a companion who could make him feel secure and protected; we dined and talked, and his confidence in me as his financial advisor in property acquisition grew over the months. Each time he traveled from his Mexican ranch to El Paso, he became more resolute about acquiring a stake in America, where his bank deposits could not be possessed by the government without warning (as they could be in Mexico, where the government federalized banks at will).

His investments in the US increased, and so did the frequency of our Vegas trips.

The Vegas floor shows were top in talent and put on consistent and varied comedy, magic, and musical productions with famous American singers. I also thoroughly enjoyed the hours of playing blackjack and Texas Hold 'em we spent together. It was work through vacationing! Vegas often accommodated my client with private jet round-trip transportation and free elite hotel rooms, so there was nothing toilsome about this line of work.

Life was good. My commissions were good. We sold our home and moved up to a more elaborate and spacious home on McFall Street. The elementary school and high school were a few blocks from our door. We installed a large backyard swimming pool, and our family had joyous swim and barbecue days with our extended family and many of our huge circle of friends visiting. We had a large den with a fireplace and hosted many parties with food and liquor and friends. Our Christmases were embellished by my wife's passion for seasonal decorating to the maximum, with house displays, a huge tree, and outside lights and visitors. We drove our girls around town on Christmas Eve to see everyone's enchanting displays.

One Christmas, when the girls were two and seven, after all the Christmas gifts were opened and the girls were playing with their new toys, Patricia said we should close our eyes and she would bring out another gift for everyone—something for the house. That was not exciting to anyone; the girls guessed between them if it was a toaster or a rake or a chair.

My wife left the living room. A couple of minutes later she reappeared, saying, "Okay, open your eyes."

We were all shocked and thrilled by what she was holding in her arms: a beautiful, black, furry, female German shepherd puppy!

We named her Wolfie, and she ended up being our family dog for twelve years. She was an extremely attentive watchdog, but also a loving pet. Patrice entered her into a dog show at the park once, and she won. Wolfie loved Tresha, and we knew she was very safe playing in the backyard under her watch. Our Thanksgivings were Norman Rockwell vintage, always with a huge turkey and my or my wife's family included. We took two family vacations each year, initially to all points of California, Florida, Canada, and Mexico, and later to Italy and Greece.

Patricia was thirty-seven when she told me she was pregnant with our third (and necessarily our last) child. I had always passionately craved a son. This was my last chance. Sex of the fetus could at this time not be discovered before the birth, so that gave me nine months to wonder, ask God to make it a boy, try not to ponder it because it was driving me nuts, stop thinking about it, and then be jarred into thinking and wondering about it. I watched my wife, trying to identify any clue that she was carrying a boy. It didn't help when she told me in her fifth month that she had another girl's name picked out: Andrea.

She was more tired carrying this baby, but she was also older, and the doctor's conjecture was that the tiredness was due to her "just being older" and that the easiest child-bearing years were the twenties, which she had well passed. I felt like I had a big bet on the roulette table and would either win all or be demolished, losing my prize of a son.

The nine months finally, agonizingly, passed, and I found myself in the pre-delivery room with Patricia. I noticed a strange signal coming from the machine to which she was attached by a sensory belt, and I called for the doctor and asked what it meant.

"That means we have to do a C-section immediately," he promptly said.

More waiting, now with serious anxiety for the safety of the baby and my wife. At least an hour passed before the doctor came out.

"You have a strong, fine-looking boy," he told me, smiling.

By God! The roulette wheel had hit! It was 1977, and every piece of my life's puzzle was assembled in place. I had to slow down my mental soaring. A boy! The boy every man must have! I was ecstatic.

The joy of taking Davy home to our daughters beat any Christmas. They were thirteen and eight years old and doted on their new baby brother. Life couldn't have been more perfect.

I played handball rigorously twice a week and was in great physical condition. My fortieth birthday came like a shockwave. I was demolished at this betrayal of my youth; I felt it had fled unexpectedly, when I had possessed, protected, and expressed it so eloquently.

Patricia talked up the event, assuring me I had just become a fully mature man; she said I was the epitome of masculine prowess and attractiveness. I eventually relaxed, and once I realized I still saw the same me in the mirror, I just went with it. Her shock would come five years later, on her fortieth, and I would weave a similar tale of assurance for her.

Life was great. We were gifted. Every day was secure, and I owned it! My earth axis was stable. Patricia and I had earned this. There was nothing but good stuff to come. We knew how to make it happen. We had the formula. It was just too sweet.

CHAPTER 28

Whipping Out Swim Laps

I WAS SWIMMING—feeling strong at forty-five years of age and sucking up the good life doing laps in our beautiful backyard pool, hearing our three kids squeal and play water games next to me. My wife brought snacks to the poolside and then lounged, enjoying the fun. My commissions from commercial real estate had by this point flourished to the extent that Patricia had quit her teaching job so she could stay home with our children.

Going into my fourth lap, I felt a burning sensation in my chest I had never experienced before. It was strong enough to make me stop swimming. Getting out of the pool and sitting down did not diminish the surge of pain.

After a while it subsided, and I called a cardiologist friend to whom I had rented a space for his medical practice in a building I managed and of which I was a 10 percent owner. It was the first prominent commercial share property I'd bought into myself.

"Come in to take a stress test," he said firmly. I felt uneasy at the urgency in his voice.

I went in the next day for the test, feeling sure I would ace it because I had been athletic all my life and was a devoted handball player, which is the maximum sport for a strenuous workout. I was confident in my health and vigor but perplexed at the burning onslaught I had just experienced.

The results of the stress test were a slapdown! My friend said I had a serious heart condition and referred me to a top heart surgeon who had studied under Dr. DeBakey, an innovator in heart surgery—specifically, a pioneer of open-heart surgery in the US.

It was a stunning blow to hear the heart surgeon say I needed immediate bypass surgery. Those were the most staggering and disconcerting words I'd ever heard. They undermined my physical prowess, which had always been my major asset—one I'd both exploited and depended upon. My strength had always been there to pull me out of any tight spot in the Navy and on the PD; now, the physical endurance and power I'd always felt I could tap into was under threat.

The hospitalization and surgery were scheduled so fast I was just pushed forward in a stupor of dread with the input of constant assurances from my family, who were disguising their own shock and foreboding. I was prepped for surgery and wheeled into the operating room in a frantic whiz of words, nurses, doctors, supportive medical machinery, and subdued panic.

My family and their hand holders waited in the adjoining room for the tortuous and interminable freezing of time as I swooned into a world of unknowing and absence of thought.

The universe had changed. I was out of the world, not knowing if I would reenter or what my plight would be if I did. It was not in my nature to be out of control and unable to manipulate my circumstance. What would I awake to—and would I ever get the steering wheel in my own hands again?

The awakening, the pain—strong, but slightly subdued by morphine. Blurry awareness that it was over. A stupor of confusion. My dad standing by my bed as I lay prostrate and immobile. Knowing I was alive. My wife, her face of love and strength injecting me with survival.

Everything moved slowly. *They want me to stand up?!* I was incredulous.

Yes, they said, to avoid blood clots.

Hours, minutes, even days and nights had no separation. I just drifted. Then I lifted my torso; then I sat up and managed to talk. Then I walked a bit down a hospital hall with attendants.

The oversight was constant for ten days. *I'm alive!* my mind yelled. I felt my leg strength kicking in. My arms worked. The surgical pain had replaced the fearful burning. My thoughts shored me up. I had been saved. It all was working. *Thank you, God. I'm back again!*

One day, Patricia brought a portable cassette player to my hospital room and lay in bed with me so we could listen to our favorite classical music and opera singers. It was the best respite from the hospital atmosphere of sick and disabled people. The most I was doing was walking down halls several times a day; my restless spirit had begun to stir. I would be discharged in a day.

Why wait in here all day? I thought. I put on my pants and shirt, unplugged the machine that monitored my heartbeat, blood pressure, and other body activity, and looked at Patricia. "Walk with me to the elevator," I said.

She had no idea that I was going to get on.

When it opened, I said, "Let's go downstairs," and she complied. Once we were downstairs, I said, "Let's go see *Blazing Saddles*. We'll be back in a couple hours."

She was like a kid skipping school; she said we shouldn't, that it wasn't allowed, but conceded at my insistence. She drove us to an indoor movie close by and we watched the film, which was hilarious. I laughed a lot and it hurt to laugh, but I didn't care: it felt great to be alive and out of the hospital.

When we stepped off the elevator to return to my room at the hospital, no one had noticed that I was gone. When I got back into the bed for my last night there, Patricia and I were amazed to realize that the nursing staff had not noticed that my plugs to the monitoring machine had been disconnected for two hours. I could have been dead and no one would have known.

It's a good time to go home, I thought.

It wasn't as over as I thought. The top of the surgical cut opened overnight to the size of a quarter my first night home, and was oozing green discharge the next morning. I was readmitted to the hospital, where the cardiologist told my wife the infection could only be defeated if it had not already spread to the bone. When she asked how we could tell if it had spread to the bone the doctor replied, "We just wait to see if he gets better or not; if the bone is infected, it will be lethal."

A full week of antibiotics and hospitalization did fix it. I went home with a whole new diet that omitted red meat and most fats and was embellished with fruits and vegetables. I also was on a cholesterol control medication.

I went after this second chance religiously. I read and absorbed with commitment a book the doctor recommended to me: *Is it Worth Dying For?* by Robert S. Eliot M.D. and Dennis L. Breo. That book turned around my approach to living, with psychological adjustments to achieve a life that was both physically and mentally balanced. I have reread it several times over the years. It has been my compass.

Patricia and I took long walks to reach the park across from Burgess High School and then we walked the park grounds. Each walk got easier as the weeks passed. The concept of death had always seemed far distant in my own life, although I had seen it many times as a cop and detective. When it surfaces as reality, you reach far to barter with it. On our walks, Patricia and I had sincere talks and promised each other that if there were an awareness or existence after death, we would find each other. It was solemn.

As I healed, the prospect of death drifted from our immediate perspective, but that did not cloud our enthusiasm for regaining our active life. The promise always remained as an understood commitment. We walked for months, and then I gradually began easing into racquetball, which was a bit less strenuous than handball but brought me back to full strength and physical fitness within a few months.

CHAPTER 29

Grabbing the World

AFTER MY SURGERY, PATRICIA got her teaching job back and never quit again. Our life got back on course, with one major change in direction: I was even more passionately driven than before by the need for financial security and pursued the acquisition of property.

Over the next few years, I bought several shopping centers with partners, investing the commissions I'd saved. I also bought some apartment buildings but found that running them was much more problematic and time-consuming than running commercial properties, which spaces are rented under lease and which tenants were much more financially secure and reliable. I expanded my business and personal relationships with my Mexican investors as well, which gave me appreciable commissions and opportunities to buy into shares of their investments. It was my best life's move. And we did move on!

Our life had become so burdened with the heavy prospect of keeping me alive, and arranging for financial security for our family in case I fell ill again. Now, we felt energetically ignited to reassemble the secure previous life before what I viewed as my passing visitor of death. We wanted our zest for life back. To recoup, Patricia arranged a three-week tour for us, beginning with a week in New York City, from which we flew across the Atlantic to Italy for another week and then to Greece for the third week, taking Davy and Tresha with us.

On our first week in New York, we stayed at a beautiful hotel downtown and got the full flavor of NYC by cab and subway, visiting all the treasures housed in the city's multitudes of historic sites. When we stepped through the massive doors of the Metropolitan Museum of Art (The Met) after our two-hour visit, Tresha paused at the top level and looked across the great, looming skyscrapers and fierce flow of the hustling crowds of people, and said breathlessly, "I'll come back here someday to stay."

And she did; we would discover later that her whole future lay therein.

We ate at a new splendid restaurant every night but were taken aback by how many hotel personnel, restaurant workers, and cab drivers issued us constant warnings not to take our hands off our children—to hold them with a firm grip at all times. Looking around, we noticed very few other children on the streets we walked—always upbeat areas of the city—and we tightened our grip. We later learned that before Rudy Giuliani became mayor, child snatching was a swift and fairly frequent occurrence in daytime Manhattan. Stepping over homeless people sleeping along the crowded sidewalks, peddlers aggressively approaching pedestrians, drunks sleeping in public view, and beggars had all become a conspicuous backdrop in the commercial area where tourists and indigenous New Yorkers walked, worked, hailed cabs, and ventured beneath the massive sidewalks to make a subway trip to their destination. It was an off-putting environment that gave a sense of lurking danger until Giuliani became mayor and began restructuring the city priorities so open access to clean and unblocked streets, sidewalks, and stairways was enforced by removing the street dwellers and promoting a greater police presence to monitor the crowds.

In massive Central Park, there was an elegant, fun restaurant called Tavern on the Green that attracted both locals and tourists. Eating there was a full evening's entertainment. The street vendors beckoned from every direction and offered great opportunities to pick up souvenirs. People played live music, sang, and danced on streets around the park and subway stations, soliciting tips. Tresha babysat Davy in the very secure hotel, with the management's knowledge and oversight, as Patricia and I went to see the popular Broadway play *Zorba the Greek*, starring Anthony Quinn. It was spectacular, and when we visited Tresha in her post-Harvard life in New York in later years, we saw many more Broadway shows, including *Chicago* (that one more than once).

On this first trip to New York, we took a two-hour river cruise to see Ellis Island, the receiving station for immigrants from all over the world, and the Statue of Liberty. We went to the top of the Empire State Building and saw the interior of the massive twin towers.

The thought often visited me during this fun, exuberant vacation, that I had almost left this world. The expertise of the hands of the heart surgeon who'd operated on me had changed that destiny. A new life. A new perspective: time no longer seemed endless. A closer caring. A touch of humility.

Patricia

On the long flight to Europe, my son would walk through the aisle and look at the passengers and start talking to them. I watched closely so I could see if the people he picked to chat with were annoyed, but they all seemed very entertained by him and even laughed with him. The airline hostesses seemed to adopt him and handed him treats to munch on.

I glanced down the aisle to keep my eye on his ventures, and suddenly I didn't see him, which caused an instant panic reflex. I knew he couldn't have left the plane, of course, and the hostesses were calmly smiling at me and I asked one of them, with a hint of frantic concern, "Where is my son?"

"Oh, the pilot let your son go into the pilot's cabin with him," she calmly and cheerfully told me.

I was startled by this. "Why?"

"The copilot asked the pilot if the little guy could step in for a minute to see how it looks from the plane's front window and to see the pilot fly the plane," she explained.

I relaxed and sat for a couple minutes, waiting for the pilot's cabin door to open and my son to reappear—and then I felt the plane take a slight but conspicuous right-angle dip, which all the other passengers also noticed. I was already lifted up, ready to go to the cabin's door, when it suddenly opened and my son rushed out, smiling excitedly. He ran straight to my seat.

"What were you doing with the pilot?" I asked.

"He let me fly the plane!" he said.

"*How*?" I asked.

He said the pilot had let him sit in his lap and had showed him what to hold and manipulate to "drive the plane."

The other passengers next to us were as astonished as I was. I looked at the hostess closest to us, who had also heard Davy's story. "Does that ever happen?"

She just smiled a bit nervously and stepped away from us, back to her serving station.

Today, years later, Davy still says he flew the plane! And yes, he laughs, it was so much fun when he got to dip the plane!

David

We toured all the historic sites in Rome and Athens and took in the music and food of the Italian and Greek cultures. We were very put off in Italy by how the men were openly aggressive and disrespectful to their women. We were also dismayed by how, when we entered a bank, there was always an armed guard behind a glass at the entrance, with a rifle pointed at the incoming customers, and no friendly greeting face. One day, walking the tourist area streets, we mistakenly turned into a street that was a bit off the main flow of tourists, and a guard with a purposely menacingly scowl uttered no words but lifted and pointed the rifle, and from a distance of only one foot, straight at the face of my wife. We quickly retreated.

The immense sculptures lining the bridge crossing the Tiber River were all male, accentuating their muscles and masculinity, and were threatening in posture. We knew who was boss. We collected some inscribed stones, which lay scattered on the unprotected grounds, from the Roman Forum, where Brutus assassinated Caesar.

The Vatican engulfed us as we toured centuries' worth of art and wealth accrued for and by the Catholic Church through the centuries of Papal control of European thrones and populations, all of which paid required tribute to the church. For centuries, from 476 to 1492 AD, any art created had to have church approval; this was rigorously enforced by the church, and any art that artists created without permission was usually destroyed on charges of blasphemy. Such indoctrination was slow to wane and explains the overabundance of religious figures and scenes filling the Vatican walls, which are embossed with gold.

The Sistine Chapel fresco laboriously created by Michaelangelo from 1508 to 1512 lavishly illustrates the artist's continued adherence to the religious doctrine imposed upon artists for over one thousand years; clearly, even after 1492, it was still a guideline to be feared. Still, no matter the motivation, the fresco is breathtaking and worth seeking out to view the mindset of medieval populations and Vatican power, elaborately expressed by the most gifted artist of the century.

The Roman Colosseum was a grim tour, a reminder of the infliction of agonizing deaths meted out to Christians for over one thousand years: slow burning, being tied to a pole during night hours to light up the Colosseum, being chased and eaten alive by lions, and other inventive methods of torture designed to excite the crowd and increase their demand for more.

Also predestined for an entertaining death were the contenders, gladiators, forced into a variety of combat or games. All life-or-death decisions were made according to the Emperor's whim, or the roar of the crowd's demands. The Colosseum is a monument to man's potential for perverse and sustained evil.

Let us not demolish it, lest we forget.

Greece was the real fun and hospitality. The crowds of Greeks mingled happily with the profuse visitors who came to see their sights and experience their culture, and they shared their music and dance with warmth, inviting visitors to jump right in and dance with them. The food was ample and delicious. The tours of the Parthenon and other past habitats of the great philosophers Aristotle, Plato, and Socrates were leisurely and fascinating; our tour guide did a wonderful job revealing the long-passed wisdom and history those men had bequeathed to the world.

We went to a beach on the Mediterranean and were surprised to discover that it was a nude beach—no one had told us this would be the case—but it was inoffensive, as all the beautiful people were wearing swim suits and only the aged and bent over bodies were actually nude, which was more comical than troublesome.

Sunbathing on this crowded beach, I ran my hands aimlessly through the sand and felt my fingers brush against an object. I dug it up from apparently being buried below the feet of many beach frequenters for a long time, and found it to be a beautiful, 18-carat gold medal of St. Francis of Assisi, in a setting and on a chain that only could have been designed for a man. I put it on, and have now worn it for thirty-seven years.

From the same beach, my son collected a batch of hermit crabs, which he boarded the plane carrying upon our return to the US.

On the long flight across the Atlantic and back to the US, I began to reminisce about Mexico and the stories my engineering friend, Dr. Elenton, had barraged me with during my university years concerning the massive, unexplored, gold-streaked mines of Mexico. He had always urged me to join him in exploring the potential fortunes lying there, not to mention enthused about the real adventures to be had there.

For the first time, I gave deep thought to the possibility of my joining this venture. I decided I would call Dr. Ellenton as soon as I got back to the States.

I did call him soon after my return, and we met to discuss a plan. In no time, we were planning the excursion. I was feeling more than physically up to it. The thought of going looking for gold mines generated excitement—both for the promise of profit and for the adventure of the quest.

CHAPTER 30

If You Want to See Old Mexico

IF YOU WANT TO see Old Mexico, ride the train from Chihuahua to the Sea of Cortez. I got on that train in 1982, at the age of forty-seven, with some investors and mining engineers looking to invest in a gold mine. We stopped at different places along the way, one of which was Copper Canyon, located high in the mountains, which is equivalent to the Grand Canyon but more beautiful. There, we bought a bunch of Indian corn bread, made of the same stuff tortillas are made of, from Tarahumara Indians, and it was the most delicious bread I had ever tasted.

Three hours later, we got off the train again at the small town of Baouchivo, a Tarahumara village and trading station, and were met by a couple of Mexicans with a dilapidated old truck. The truck's wooden bed barely held the ten of us, but somehow we got into Sirakowi, populated with about two hundred Tarahumaras who lived in dirt-floored adobe huts—shacks with little trails all around them—with a pile of corn and a pile of beans in front of every hut. The people were moon-faced and very shy and passive; the tallest person was four-foot-five. They spoke no English or Spanish, so we had to get an interpreter, an Indian who spoke both Tarahumara and Spanish, at the Catholic Church in the center of the town.

Inside the church, built by Spanish Conquistadores, you could see where all the gold had been removed by pilferers, leaving chunk marks in walls. There was a corner stone in the church with a date of 1697. We asked our translator to get us a couple of women to do our cooking, get together a corn and bean supply, and be ready to go at daylight for our four-hour horseback journey into the rugged, pine tree–covered mountains.

We arrived to our lodging area—two uninhabited adobe huts with Indian-type stoves, a couple of outhouses in back, and a basic corral made of logs for horses, all of which belonged to our fellow traveler and mine owner, Jake Vasquez—at 2:00 p.m. Our party of ten, which included two *pistoleros* as guards and Professor Ellenton of UTEP, who was carrying maps and assays of the mine from the 1930s (they had been validated by other professionals), tried to keep warm in the cold using bedrolls Jake had furnished, only to find that some had lice. We sat around the fire in the cooking hut while the women boiled beans and corn and made tortillas and eggs for our breakfast. This was our diet for five days; not tasty, but palatable.

Around sunset, we sat out in the cold open air, and talked about how to assay the mine. At one point, I got up and walked over to one of the guards, Jesus, who was sitting close by.

"*Hablas Español?*" I asked.

He nodded, so I asked him in Spanish if I could see his rifle. As I looked down the barrel, I saw that it was bent by about two inches; the barrel veered rather sharply to the right. It was an old WWI Springfield rifle, which is what had drawn me to him in the first place—I'd immediately recognized it.

"How do you expect to be a guard and protect us with a rifle like this?" I asked him.

"At close range, I'm very accurate," he said convincingly.

I picked out a bottle, walked a hundred paces, set it on the ground, and asked him to demonstrate his accuracy.

He kneeled, took aim, pointed the rifle a bit to the left of the target to accommodate the veering to the right he knew the bullet would do, fired, and—to my surprise—hit the bottle dead center.

I noticed that his right thumb was missing. "What happened to your thumb?" I asked.

"It was shot off by a bandit that hides out in the mountains near here." He pointed to some smoke about half a mile from our camp. "Those are the bandits there."

I pulled out my binoculars and stared into their binoculars, looking back at me. He handed me the rifle for me to shoot, and I took my shot and missed.

"Look," I said, "this gun will only be good to shoot a hundred feet, being so old and filthy." I still remembered my gunner's mate training from the navy, so I told him to give me some oil, even cooking oil, and I'd take it apart and try to clean it. Hopefully, I could clean it enough that it wouldn't rot—it was loaded with rust. I also asked for a metal saw to chop the barrel down so it wouldn't be crooked.

While I was disassembling the gun, I noticed parts missing. After I put it back together, I handed it to Jesus and said, "This is all I can do with it. Be careful, because it will backfire on you." The barrel was still crooked, and I felt so sorry for him that I gave him my business card. "Look, if you're ever in Juarez, Mexico, call me at this number and I will give you a really good rifle," I promised. In the meantime, I told him not to confront his enemy across the hill, because he would probably get his other thumb shot off.

We took the four horses loaned to us by villagers and our two donkeys, which we loaded with supplies, and started up a rugged path with pine trees encroaching onto the trail. The trail weaved upward and downward at sharp angles; about four hours and two hundred feet later, we reached the mine. There were two empty huts near the mine that belonged to our companion, Jake Vasquez. He unlocked them for our stay.

Our objective was to accumulate a load of quartz in two large potato sacks to take to El Paso, where we would assess what quantity of gold was in the quartz. With miners' hats with lamps on them and holding flashlights, two Indians, Dr. Ellenton, and I entered the mine, which was five feet high and five feet in diameter. We followed the readily apparent shiny, whitish vein of quartz. The Indians were carting small buckets of water in a rail cart about three feet deep; they dragged them along the old, preexisting rails. Each cart could hold 150 to 200 pounds of rock. We needed the water to rinse the dust off the vein so we could see the gold, and thus know where to make our cuts.

We penetrated the mine for about an hour, with the Indians sporadically rinsing the veins, until we arrived at a juncture in the mine where another horizontally running vein crossed the vein we had been following. There was also a ten-foot-wide hole, full of rain water that had flooded into the mine in previous months, at the juncture. The rails stopped at the hole, then picked up again at the other side.

We were using old maps Vasquez had given us that had been drawn by an American metallurgist from Colorado College of Mines in the mid-1930s. The map drawer had been Vasquez's partner, but had been drafted into the US Army in WWII and gotten killed in that war.

Dr. Ellenton stared at the seemingly impassable waterhole. "Let's sit down and have something to drink and a sandwich," he said.

As we ate, Dr. Ellenton told me that the crossing veins were a very important find. "Someone dug this hole on purpose," he said, "so this area would flood and keep explorers out. When two veins cross, that's considered the glory hole—a prime place to find the most gold." He then asked me if I'd be willing to dive down into the bottom of the hole to bring back a bucket of silt.

Before I jumped in, we tied a rock to the end of a rope and threw it into the water to assess the depth of the hole. It looked to be about ten to twelve feet.

"I can go that deep easily," I said. I took off my clothes, tucked a waterproof lamp under my armpit, picked up a bucket of rocks to help me descend, and jumped in.

I plunged quickly to the bottom. Guessing I could hold my breath for a minute, I moved as fast as possible, first dumping the rocks and then quickly scraping the bucket over the bottom of the waterbed. After I'd scooped up about half a bucket of silt, I pulled on the rope for help ascending.

After bringing the first bucket of silt up, I repeated the feat twice more, with more assuredness on these attempts due to the warmth of the water and the ease of my first jump. After the third jump, I dried off as much silt and mud as I could with my T-shirt and put my clothes back on. Next, we sent the Indians back to retrieve two trees we'd seen outside the mine that had been chopped down long ago. We used the trees as a bridge across the water hole, and they were a perfect fit—which made us wonder if they had been cut for that very purpose.

We walked easily across the tree bridge, and continued our efforts, gouging out pieces of quartz and marking each spot with a can of blue spray paint.

We numbered the vein and the rocks to match all the way through until we came to another juncture about one hundred feet farther along that split the mine in two different directions. We followed the vein to the right because it seemed larger. The mine narrowed, and soon we were reduced to traveling on our hands and knees. There was a light about fifty feet ahead, and I pressed along toward it.

Suddenly, a sharp object hit my knee. I felt around and held it up in front of my light to see what it was—and lifted up an old Spanish spur. I stuck it between my belt and waist and continued until we reached another mine opening large enough to walk out through.

A few feet below this exit were the remains of four or five old rock huts with an old mill in the center, the type the Spanish used to grind down quartz. The mill was oval shaped, with a huge rock about three feet tall and five feet long and with a hole in the middle for a wooden axel, which we found rotted inside the rock.

Dr. Ellenton explained that the Spanish employed this method to separate the ore from the quartz, taking as much gold as possible. They'd left the tailings on the side of the huts, which were still standing. I felt, at that moment, that I had leapt back in time three hundred years and could visualize Indians much like the men in our group performing this labor under Spanish supervision.

As we sat outside the mine, Dr. Ellenton explained, at length, the culture of the unique times, the people, and their mining methods, which created the ruins we had found, and which had been deserted for unknown reasons at least three hundred years earlier. The place's isolated quiet made it the most impressive museum I've ever been to.

We rested by the huts for about half an hour. While Dr. Ellenton educated us, I washed off the silver spur I'd found, which appeared to be a unique Spanish artifact. When we were ready to move on, we went back into the mine opening from which we had exited and backtracked, picking up our tailings and silt, which we had left in the mine in the rail car, along the way.

It took us about forty-five minutes to reach the opening from which we had started. When we stepped out into the daylight, there stood Jesus, his rifle on his shoulder, standing at attention and guarding the mine during our absence—a loyal soldier. It was comical but reassuring, his wanting us to know that he was earning his money with alert diligence; it reminded me of Don Quixote.

We dumped all our rocks on a tray, and Dr. Ellenton took out an oval-shaped wooden board that looked like a rat maze. He poured the silt I'd brought up from the water hole onto it and poured cans of water into the top of the maze. The water and silt moved around in many circular paths as it worked its way down, the silt separating from the gold. As the water and silt flowed down the hole at the bottom, they left gold deposits behind on the platform pathways.

Seeing the gold, I suddenly experienced "gold fever" and wanted to rush back in to get more. We made two more (better organized and swifter) trips into the mine, retrieved two more large buckets full of silt from the bottom of the water hole, and repeated the separating process outside the mine—this time in the seclusion of a newly erected tent for secrecy. We were all amazingly tireless.

After three nights, though our zest and greed for our gold expedition was strong, our dwindling food supply and our investors' need to return to their businesses stateside forced us to abandon any further search. This was expedited by the investors' deteriorating state: they had quickly tired of waiting for us on our first mine excursion, and had sent the Indians back to their village to retrieve alcohol. The Indians gladly accommodated them, and returned with the only liquor: a 200-proof drink called Tamures. The investors soon became so falling-down drunk, belligerent, and hard to handle that we had to immediately cancel the trip. Their spontaneous sexual advances toward the shy Indian women who had come with us as cooks could have caused an extreme wrathful reaction by the Indian men.

My great exuberance upon our return from this trip quickly turned to shock when I discovered that I had lost the treasure of my Spanish spur. This brought me serious anguish; however, my pain over the loss was assuaged by the two ounces of gold dust we brought back to the US. Dr. Ellenton and I split the money we got from an El Paso jeweler for the gold at our trip's end.

About four months later, I got a strange call at my office:

"Hello," a man said in Spanish, "are you Mr. Rodriguez, the one who went up to Vasquez's mine?"

"Yes," I said, a little confused.

"This is Jesus," he burst out excitedly, "and I've come for the rifle you promised me."

I vaguely remembered making this offer. "How come it took you so long to get here?" I asked.

"Because I walked to Juárez all the way from Sirucoui, Chihuahua, to get here," he replied. "It took me four months."

I asked him, a bit astonished, if he'd made the walk in the Indian huaraches he'd worn for the climb to the mine, which were cut-up old tire treads tied to his feet and around his ankles by leather strips. He said he had.

Uncomfortably, I had a surge of wanting to keep my rifle; I truly hadn't believed at my moment of offering it that Jesus would ever show up. But after hearing his story of his grueling, 300- to 400-mile journey with no money and sparse food, I readily agreed to meet him in Juarez.

I went home and took my WWII M-I Carbine rifle out of my gun case, wrapped it with newspaper, and threw it into the trunk of my car, along with two banana clips of ammunition, then drove to the border and met Jesus at 16th of September Street and Lervo.

He looked eager, thin, and shabby, and brought with him the rancid smell of an arduous journey when he climbed into my car. I drove to a little Mexican restaurant about two blocks away and ordered him a full meal, including a huge T-bone steak. The owners of the restaurant were very good friends of mine, so they let us use a private room where I could talk to Jesus alone. I took the rifle from the car to the back room and showed it to him. He was so happy when he grasped it that he started crying. I showed him how to break the rifle down to clean it and how to load and take care of it. Along with the ammo, I gave him a can of gun oil and cleaning rods. We spent about two hours talking about the mines, his family, and how broke he was. I knew he was totally sincere because of the incredible walk he'd made to get the rifle, which he would use as a hunting rifle to increase his family's food supply and as a weapon, which would get him more employment as a guard.

I asked Jesus how he was going to get home.

"I'll walk back, the same way I came," he said simply.

I gave him twenty dollars. "Ride the bus to Chihuahua, and then catch the train home," I said.

He humbly put the money into his pocket and, with a choked voice, expressed much gratitude.

"Come on," I said. "I'll take you to the bus station."

"Please sir, understand, I cannot spend this money on a bus; I need it for my family, and I can walk back just the way I came."

Defeated by his reasoning, I took him to the bus station, bought him a non-refundable bus ticket to Chihuahua, and added another twenty dollars to his pocket cash. Everything about this struggling, valiant man had me close to tears. I told him that when I saw him again at the mines in a few months, I expected to hear from him that he had shot off the bandit's thumb who had shot off his own thumb.

He grinned. "Sí!"

I saw him board the bus and we waved good-bye. The last words I heard him say were, "*Que Dios te bendiga*," meaning "May God bless you."

I had a quadruple heart bypass operation at age forty-five. Once I'd recuperated enough to travel, I tried the mine trip again with Dr. Ellenton and two new Mormon investors out of Arizona. We felt secure that they would not give us the lecherous and drunken problems the previous investors had, and these men had the money to erect a mill to process the gold.

We got to the mine by the same accommodations and travel route as we had the first trip, and I requested Jesus as a bodyguard. When we saw each other, he hugged me and shook my hand, looking very grateful and confident with his new rifle. His sixteen-year-old son went with us this time as well; I was surprised to see him using his dad's old crooked Springfield rifle, but with the barrel chopped down so it shot straight.

With the same mine reports we had assayed on the previous trip in hand, we made more cuts to the new investors' satisfaction, which samples they took to Arizona. After we all returned home, their assay came out exactly the same as ours: two ounces of gold per ton of quartz. A month later, they called me in El Paso to sign a lease for the mine with Jake Vasquez, who held the primary lease. He subleased it to the Mormons, and recorded an agreement in Mexico City that gave them permission to erect a mill. They did so when we returned three months later, at a cost of over $300,000.

The lease terms were for the Mormons to pay Jake Vasquez 15 percent of the gross profits of the mine. I was to receive 2 percent. Upon completion of the mill, they hired Tarahumara Indians to cut into the veins and do the mining. The mill chopped the quartz the Indians extracted into smaller pieces, and these were sent to Asarco in Chihuahua City to be separated. After separation, the government got a share of 25 percent of the gold; the remaining balance, after separation costs, was given to the Mormons. My 2 percent came from Jake Vasquez.

Business was started, with great expectations, and I left, assuming I would return soon.

The process continued smoothly for six months, consistently yielding two ounces per ton. Then the Mexican government increased its share to more than 50 percent. The Mormons went to complain to the Mexican government officials that the new share split was unfair, and two days later one of them was found dead, a bullet hole through his head, in a back alley in Chihuahua. The other partner immediately boarded a plane back to Arizona, leaving his invested money and mill to the mercy of the Mexican mining unions—which, without employers or directors, disassembled the mill and sold the parts. The mine disintegrated.

Again I remembered how my dad had left Mexico in 1915 as a young adult during the Mexican Revolution. He'd left because of the brutality and corruption of the federal government, and to find employment in America. The Revolution clearly hadn't decreased the corruption and unquestioned power of the federal government. This unsolved murder, along with the government's unpredictable intrusion into the mine's profits, re-impressed upon me the futility of trusting business investing in Mexico at that time. It also cured my gold fever.

I reflected on my friend Jesus often in the days after the mine was shut down, but I never saw or heard from him again. It took me a while to quit picturing him and wondering about his life with his new rifle. Gradually he took his place in the past, but occasionally I still think of him and his desperation and determination to survive. That's why now, after twenty-nine years, I feel compelled to write his story down.

Jesus's plight was a repetition of my own father's experience of traveling through Mexico sixty-seven years earlier. My father didn't journey by foot, but he too was in search of a better life, away from the corruption, pillaging, and life-threatening conditions of the Revolution and the dictatorship it sought to unseat.

CHAPTER 31

Silk, Slugger, Spice, Sad

David

All my life, adventure meant leaving home to find it. That's what took me to train hopping and the oceans of the Navy bringing the endless mix of excitement, ecstasy, unplanned and unforeseen adventure, even unwanted trauma. Our realm of adventure expanded unpredictably and explosively as our four children came a few years apart and consumed us with the love, energy, and adventure they all manufactured on their own. It was a keep up game with excitement, fun, anxiety, and devastation which we learned were the usual ingredients of parenting. In we jumped.

Silk

It was five years after my full recovery from heart surgery that we received a spontaneous gift: our granddaughter, Nicole. Patrice brought her to our home after her birth, and she lived with us sporadically for her first three years

Nicole, beautiful and in love

Nicole

of life before officially and permanently becoming ours at the age of three. By then, she was already deeply embedded in our hearts, and she blended in happily as the children's sister and our new daughter; we were happy to raise and love her as a full member of our nuclear family.

I did, however, feel my age was enhanced when I heard "Grandpa!" ring out daily. "Grandpa" didn't fit in with the image of youth I tried to nurture.

One day I said, "Nicole, honey, call me Dad, like the other kids."

"But my friends know you're not my dad," she said. She thought intently for just about three minutes, and then said joyously, "I think I'll call you Peaches."

That sounded kind of young and cozy, and she had definitely lifted it from one of her furry pets, but it was better than being officially designated as a grandpa. And I nicknamed her "Peanuts" in return.

The adhesive power of Nicole's nickname for me has never lifted; people always grin or smile when they hear her earnestly address me as "Peaches." It caught on so fast that soon, when my poker player friends called my house to get a game going, they started to ask my wife, "Is Peaches there?" Even Patricia called me "The Peach."

That name will always ring more precious than Grandpa ever could have.

When Nicole was in middle elementary school, she became a cheerleader for the West Side Cowboys, a young boys' city team on which my son David played. She was performance prone, like Tresha, and made lifelong friends in her young school years. In high school, she was so entrancing to the boys her age that she often had boyfriends leaving flowers at her front door, sometimes simultaneously.

Nicole was very social and gregarious, had no puberty or teenage adjustment phases, and didn't even need braces. She was the image to live up to, with a personality as smooth as silk and an exquisitely beautiful face; she was a loving girl who everyone wanted to be around. In her senior year, she was a high school cheerleader and Lady-in-Waiting Princess at the Senior Homecoming, following three years of being voted class favorite. Everyone loved Nicole.

Basketball was her official sport in her first three years of high school, and she drew audiences attracted by her skilled, aggressive playing and beauty to every game. I instructed her early in her game not to put the ball on the floor and risk it being taken from her, but rather to shoot it at the basket at first chance every time. She followed this strategy, and was a high scorer. Nicole attended college in Denton, Texas, where she was involved in her sorority and went on several college trips of adventure to New Orleans. We visited her several times at school, and were there for her initiation into her sorority. Her Denton apartment was beautifully decorated, including with pink satin drapes of her choice. She was home for every holiday and during the summer, when the whole family gathered for barbecues and fun. Her room in our house is still in her flowery décor. After graduating college, she became an elementary school teacher, and was soon in demand with all the parents, each of them determined to secure her as their own child's teacher. She has always been an artist and has created many beautiful paintings, one of which hangs, professionally framed, in our living room.

Slugger

As my son, David, grew into his school years, I took him often up into the massive Franklin Mountains, where we looked for artifacts of past sea life, which were abundant there and which he collected with relish. These were the same mountains I had climbed for many years as a young boy before I went to Mexico and after, when I returned to El Paso two years later.

My boyhood home was located in the central area of El Paso, a part of town that dated back to the age of the original indigenous Indian inhabitants and the later gunslingers, settlers, and, eventually, US Army soldiers who established outposts there. All comers were settling and claiming the Southwest territory through strife and war. Over two centuries, the settlement areas expanded into a downtown commercial center inescapably surrounded by the intriguing mountains I had scaled with my young friends, searching open ancient caves, disregarding all danger in the excitement of adventure and the seeking of unknown treasure or historic leftovers from the many earlier conquerors. I wanted David to have an understanding of this recent human history, but also the historical and geological history of the area—the millions of years of evolution that had gone into converting the seabed on which we climbed into the massive Franklin Mountains, which had a length of twenty-three miles and width of three miles and extended through Texas and New Mexico.

I educated my son about what I knew: Faults formed within the range dated from forty-five to eighty-five million years ago. Continuous erosion had left a crumbling rock slide, mixed with sand that was once rock, covering the surface. Sea life fossils were abundant, and we spent hours searching and sifting through the surface soil—a

Always in the fight game

Constant workouts

The lure of boxing

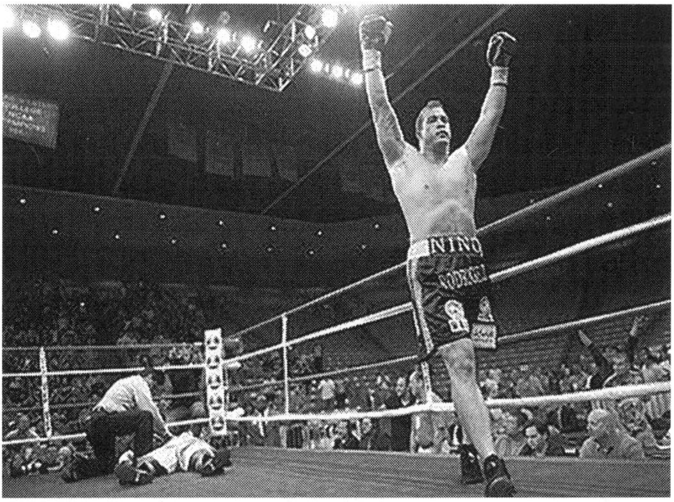

Another knock-out

time-consuming process that sometimes yielded nothing. Hours of persistent search over frequent trips eventually uncovered priceless fossils dating to origins of the earth's oceans, however. Our collection grew. Davy had become a skilled negotiator of the crumbly earth, and moved as surely and quickly as a desert scorpion.

On a fair-weather day—no blistering sun beating down—we extended our search to a higher point that did not have quite so much silt-like erosion and that we could move through with surer footing. Keeping a diligent eye on my son's position and safeness, I stepped to the edge of a ravine for a look off the side of the mountain to the left—and felt my body tilt and drop toward the steep drop below, a plunge of hundreds of feet that would end with jagged rocks.

It happened in a second: as I tilted in terror on the edge, trying to make my body retreat, but with no footing to help me, my arms flailed and grasped only air; my nine-year-old son reached fast as lightning with a powerful fist, grabbed the front of my shirt, and yanked me back to flat ground.

We lay there and stared at each other, both realizing that this simple slip had had a signature of sure death. Finally, I straightened, and we descended to a safer level.

"Son," I said, "you saved my life."

"Yeah Dad," he responded with relief.

He took the same powerful fist and quick reflexes into the boxing ring twelve years later, and used them to safeguard his own life.

I often took Davy riding on the back of my bicycle, and he and I pitched tents for him to sleep out in the backyard with his rowdy young guy friends. Like my friends and I had, they climbed trees, roamed the desert, and did daredevil moves like jump from our rooftop into our backyard pool. Davy was an adventurer, and I completely related.

He took up boxing at the age of five. He had his first amateur fight in Las Cruces, New Mexico, as a teenager, and was pitted against a formidable opponent. We attended with clenched fists.

Patricia

Steady, impenetrable eyes, a solid, square jaw, and sculpted masculine features caught the crowd's attention as the six-foot-five, sixteen-year-old heavyweight stepped between the ropes of the ring for his first public amateur fight. He would be fighting against a nineteen-year-old Junior Olympics champion boxer of the same height, who looked assured of a victory. The known champion sported a mustache that emphasized his manhood and raised his gloves high, promising the crowd a win.

The crowd was impressed and dismayed by the confidence and fitness of the younger contender. Did he know what he was stepping into?

The bell sparked the Olympic champion to come forth with a quick infliction of blows, as if he was determined to show how he'd become a champion, but he couldn't floor his young opponent. The second round brought a stunning rebuttal by the young fighter, who charged with fury, displayed his skillful power, and claimed a KO in round two. He was in to stay. He jumped onto the ropes with fists up in victory, muscled arms sweaty—a Greek warrior, thrilling the crowd.

This was a position our son repeatedly claimed for twenty years, as he was alert, devious, and precise in assessing his opponent's weaknesses within seconds of the fight's opening.

In boxing, a timid, careful guy can't win. A pompous, self-absorbed, and overly confident guy can't win. But a guy with an obsessed determination, extreme dedication to his training, and passionate mission to attack and plunder—a kamikaze fighter—can win.

David

My wife and I traveled often to see David's fights throughout the US and Mexico. It was a glorious endeavor for him. He won six championship belts and had a 36-0 fight record, with 24 KOs in the first round and 34 total KOs, before his career was cut short.

David—known as "Nino" in the boxing world—had just left a pizza parlor and was walking alone on an empty street in Scottsdale, Arizona, when he was quietly and quickly surrounded by several adult males. They demanded money; he refused. He saw the glint of a knife in his left field of vision and quickly turned his head in a duck, but the knife wielder found his target and sliced David's jaw from his ear to his chin.

David's friend, seeing and hearing the confrontation from a short distance, raced forward bravely to try to assist the champion and took several stab wounds to his arms.

As the gang disbanded and ran, David fell in the street, blood gushing forth through his face wound. His last thought before he lost consciousness was that he was about to meet his death.

A young lady who saw the attack from the parlor window raced over to David and tied a scarf tightly around his neck, stunting the blood flow just enough to allow him to hang on to life.

God allowed a master surgeon to be on call that night. Before he was released, the surgeon told David that he was lucky it was his on call night at the hospital, as the wound was a death slice that only someone with his years of expertise in surgery could have dealt with successfully. By any estimation, he said, David should not have lived through the night.

Within a couple days, David could barely talk through the pain. The recovery was long and the victim dispirited. He left town with some friends a few days later, and drove with them to another city to attend an event they had all planned before the attack—he had far underestimated the severity of the pain, having just been taken off a morphine drip. He spent the days at the event in excruciating agony.

Still, when his friends told him he should never box again, David looked at them in disbelief. Where would they have gotten a notion like that? He trained and struggled to regain his former strength and fitness, and—most crucial to possess—his self-esteem and bold confidence. He found it nearly impossible to recoup his former glory, but rebounded sufficiently to take three more fights. Today, he continues to eye the ring with serious intent. His spirit is undefeatable.

My son had experienced two episodes of knowing he was dying and being unable to reach for help. Was this to be his life, always dodging a ring bludgeoning or sudden death? Would the fast-forward thrust of every chapter be so against the wind and uncertain, after so many ring victories? Where was the anchor?

How do I find it? This question stirred David's spirit and made his sleep uneasy. Pondering and meditating over it evolved into writing his experiences down. In one swift month, using his cell phone, he wrote an intriguing and masterful book, all told in first person. The narrative pulls the reader into the story, making him captive to living each thought, feeling, joyous surge, and agony of David's life thus far. David wraps his audience into being personally involved in his flamboyant adventures, world travels, womanizing, fast friends, and the drought that follows death as one searched for a future direction. After so many ring victories, he asks in his book, where else could he look for that height of spirit that comes with the chase?

A previously unexpressed talent—compelling story writing—engulfed David. Did he know what a spontaneous, on-demand story-teller his dad had been as a kid, or how he'd been called upon to entertain his classmates with stories that he would improvise as he went?

He didn't have to know. It was genetic.

His knock-out book was published as *When the Lights Go Out*—a living biography by David Rodriguez.

A doctor bought one hundred books outright.

Spice

Tresha—"Short Pants," as I named her, because she was always in shorts—and I had a special handshake we created when she was just six, which had quick finger rotations ending in a fist bump. In grade school and junior high, she used her mattress as her first stage, singing into an imaginary microphone before an imaginary audience.

Throughout high school and college, we sat in the great McKelligon Canyon, surrounded by massive mountains

Tresha, always onstage

Tresha

under the night stars, watching Tresha splash the stage with fervor and excitement, living the musical story of the early Southwest cowboys, ranchers, Indians, Mexican Revolutionaries, bars, gambling, gunfighters, and hookers, in the summer-long production of *Viva El Paso*. She danced and sang center stage, igniting the audience with her svelte figure and classic beauty. She could emulate the full spectrum of human emotions through heavy drama or light comedy; whatever role she played, she always held the center stage and the audience's unswerving eyes.

In university, Tresha continued her pursuits onstage and won the 1991 University Players Outstanding Performance Award for best actress. In local theatre, she performed the lead female role in *Jack the Ripper*, a dark comedy at the Adobe Horseshoe Dinner Theatre, which always packed full for her performances. Her degree was in history but her heart was in acting.

Tresha created her first children's acting school in our home's massive living room, which had a circular built-in sofa for parents to marvel as they watched their children's budding acting acumen develop—a feat for which they happily paid, giving Tresha substantial income.

Tresha's zest for the stage led her to back-to-back entertainment and travel. We saw so many Treshas onstage, as she could magically transform herself into any completely believable character. She competed for acceptance and was chosen by Harvard's American Repertory Theatre, from which stage she originated the role of Suzanne in the first play Steve Martin wrote and directed, *Picasso at the Lapin Agile*. We were often in Boston to see her performances.

Two years of Harvard's rigorous acting instruction catapulted Tresha to New York, where she expressed her love of stage on Broadway in *Circus Life* and on screen in numerous television roles: *Law & Order, Kiss the Girls, The Magic Stone*, and *One Life to Live.* Her return to New York had fulfilled the prophesy she'd proclaimed on the steps of the Metropolitan Museum of New York ten years earlier on our European trip: "I will come back here."

Her theater life in Boston and NYC also prompted a love of overseas travel—a hobby that filled her young years. When a gentleman influenced her to get involved in real estate, she was hired to work at Trump Tower for Donald Trump's real estate organization, but her heart was always owned by the theatre.

Tresha consumed life with zest and vigor, and embarked on travels that took her to Cambodia, Thailand, Mexico, Canada, Italy, Greece, France, and Russia for a month, during which time the enchantment of Moscow and Saint Petersburg led her to accept a spontaneous kiss from a stalwart, impressive young Russian man, the romance of which was enhanced by moonlight flooding St. Petersburg's Palace Square.

She generated joy, deep love, and a passion for life that gifted her family with entertainment and an eternal love for her.

Sad

Patrice, our firstborn, was a girl who gestured on the playground to any kid who was left out to come join the group. "Puppy" was her first word; she always had one by her side and in her bed. She was a writer of plays in elementary school, and she cast Tresha in the central roles. She invited neighbors and friends to be the backyard audience. She was Tresha's first director and the instigator of Tresha's

Patrice's days of beauty

growing passion for acting. Her enthusiasm to decorate elaborately was her passion, so Christmas was always ecstasy for her. She was an A student with extraordinary and frequently commented-upon beauty. She also loved to ride on the back of my motorcycle. All was fun. All was loving. All was in control.

A sporadic and unexplained sadness began to surface in Patrice when she was in the fourth grade. Doctors shrugged it off. Her mother explored it reading, searching for guidance and information from books related to depression like *Speaking of Sadness* and *Sugar Blues*, which referenced the insatiable compulsion to consume sugar. None of the physicians we went to seemed to be aware of or capable of attending to childhood encroaching depression and its signature symptoms. We swam alone.

At seventeen, Patrice married and had a baby girl, Nicole—the fulfillment of a deep desire she had to have her own baby. She was entranced with the baby girl and swooned over her beauty. She coddled her attentively, dressing her for Halloween, having birthday parties with a piñata full of candy, which Nicole and her friends burst, sending sweet treats scattering on the ground that they scrambled after.

The initial marriage bliss dissolved and thus ended. Her need for friends and an independent life engulfed her and became her sole focus. She worked in my real estate office as a secretary.

After a few years, she married again. She was a beautiful bride. Nicole was her flower girl and I danced with her at the gala reception my wife arranged. It was a start-over. Nicole became legally one of our own, as Patrice assigned us, her grandparents, as legal guardians. Patrice wanted her little girl to have the security and embellished life that she could not provide. Her depression deepened. She poured herself into her animals and home décor, kept many friends, and won the first-place prize for her exterior Halloween decorations at the apartment complex to which she had moved. She cheered for her brother at every boxing match she could attend. She loved family birthdays and all holidays and was the first to arrive to join the party and celebrate the occasion. She bought gifts for everyone and loved to sing birthday praises. She wrote commemorating poems.

This poem was written by Patrice for her mother's birthday, and given to her at our customary family birthday dinner at The Bella Napoli Italian restaurant, where we often dined and enjoyed the pianist, as well as the talented vocalists who sang with him, entertaining us with a variety of classic opera, Italian, and romantic songs. My wife framed the poem, so it remains forever her own "touch of Patrice":

HAPPY BIRTHDAY MOTHER

As the chilly October wind blew,
A child was born, and it was you,
Right away your parents knew,
Your name would be Patricia Sue.
Well hello Patricia Sue.
You added a Rodriguez too,
And had some children, a few,
Two of which are named after you.
As the witching holidays draw near,
It becomes so very clear,
Your birthday is not a date to fear.
I love you Mother Dear.
—*Patrice 2000*

As the years passed, Patrice became ill and dispirited. She had lost her burden but also her compass. Her sickness became severe, ravaging and sucking out her strength and will to live. Her beauty became a memory. Her last breath was our lasting agony. Life and the world around us kept racing.

CHAPTER 32

The Big Bang of Mexico

UNTIL THE 1970S DAWNED, Mexico was America's most frequented escape country. It had everything to offer, regardless of one's age or income level. You would never be asked your age to order a drink, as long as you could reach up to the bar! The closest and therefore easily accessible city for tourists from Texas was Juarez, with its beacon floodlight of fun.

The sister city of my town, El Paso, Juárez saw heavy daily tourist travel and population exchange. Before drug production and distribution from Mexico to the US became sophisticated and organized by drug cartels, Americans flooded from all parts of their country to indulge in the luxury of food, liquor, and entertainment served lavishly and inexpensively in Juarez. In my youth and through the 1960s, before the drug cartels' takeover, all eyes looked to Juarez. El Paso was in a dry county, so no open-to-the-public places of dining or any other kind of entertainment could serve mixed drinks (though beer and wine were allowed). The many nightclubs in Juárez filled the void and flourished.

It was the place to go for elegant dinners, dancing, and shopping, and was relatively safe—factoring in the known danger of getting into the sights of a Juárez cop, as you would very likely be extorted for cash to avoid being arrested for any simple traffic violation or misbehavior loosely construed by the arresting cop. (No one could fail to be shocked by the unaccommodating atmosphere of a Juárez jail, and the danger that lurked in being there.)

Juárez and El Paso cops had a generally reciprocal unwritten code of respect for each other; I never wore my uniform there, but I often carried my badge, and that was protection against any hassle that could occur. Over time, I personally came to know many of the Juárez cops. Every year, the Juárez police force was given an appreciation *fiesta* to which an open invitation was extended to the El Paso policemen. I attended more than once, as did many of my fellow officers, and it was a rollicking social event full of mariachi, food, and liquor. El Paso custom agents were also invited, and my good friend who was with US Customs, and who had extensive involvement with investigating the smuggling of drugs to and from Mexico across the border, often attended with me. We got to be good friends over the years with a captain of the Mexican State Police—who may have bought his job, as many cops there did, but was an honest man in whom we both had confidence.

State police in Mexico ranked higher than the municipal police and had power and influence over municipalities. The Captain gave me a card to carry as protection against police of any rank who might attempt to question or detain me. The card stated that the Captain would vouch for me in any instance, and that he should be contacted in my regard in any event of concern. Despite all its tourist hospitality,

Juárez still held extreme danger for tourists, who had no constitutional rights under Mexican law and could be held unaccounted for, jailed without hearings, or just disappeared. Most partying or shopping tourists stayed on the main streets and frequented what they presumed were safe areas. The danger of being stopped or arrested without cause was always hovering. Most tourists learned to carry cash to convince any cop who detained them to excuse whatever offense for which the cop had apprehended them. It was routine business in Juarez, and visitors knew to be prepared.

A few years into my friendship with the Captain, I learned a car had recently been driven across the Juárez free bridge and abandoned on the American side of the bridge. The driver had rapidly exited the car and darted back across the bridge in a rapid return to Mexican soil. The US border agents witnessing the abandoned, apparently empty, car, searched it and, upon forcing open the trunk, found the bodies of the Captain and his two young sons. They had all been shot to death, and the Captain's hand had been cut off with the fingers left attached. The fingers were shoved into the captain's mouth—a Mexican statement that meant, "You fingered me" or "You pointed me out." It seemed the Captain had exposed someone responsible for a criminal endeavor and this was his punishment, as well as a warning to any other authority who may try to track or obstruct the same criminal.

The undercurrent of crime was always present in Juarez, as it is in any society, but it was not often displayed in such a brutal and bragging manner. Such deaths were not often presented so publicly, so the Captain's murder was meant as a ruthless and serious warning to diminish the enthusiasm of pursuit among all law enforcement personnel. I'm sure it was effective.

CHAPTER 33

The Nightlife

I OFTEN CROSSED OVER the Bridge of the Americas, which closed the natural gap between America and Mexico by providing a pathway for pedestrians and automobiles across the Rio Grande River, which was the designated border line between El Paso and Juarez. Many people parked their cars stateside and walked across the bridge, always marveling in sympathy at the many children and young adults standing knee- or waist-deep in the water below, holding long poles with drooped open nets attached, begging for passing tourists to drop some coins into their nets. Their success of actually catching the small coins from the considerable distance from which they were flung looked unachievable, but the beggars had honed their skill to a high degree of accuracy for which the tourists cheered.

Many tourists drove into Juárez and parked on the street; their car's safety was secured by paying one of the many young Mexican boys who eagerly offered to guard their car for a small amount of change, which was to be paid when the owner returned and saw the car had not been stolen or damaged. This system was very reliable, and it was also a reliable fact that if a driver did *not* hire one of the boys, the car would highly likely sustain some injury or even theft.

The excitement of Juárez reached your ears as soon as you reached the midpoint of the bridge, as loud mariachi music bellowed invitingly from open bars on nearby corners. Mariachis are groups of three to five male singers with guitars who wear the customary, colorful, ranch-inspired costumes and huge sombreros of Mexican balladeers. An occasional woman would be in the group and always contributed a sterling and powerful high-pitched voice. The ballads' lyrics were of Old Mexican history or heroes, ranch songs, or songs of the Revolution, and were endlessly romantic.

Along with the music, a ready profusion of liquor was served at the standing-room-only bars and at the tables where couples sat waiting, thirsty for Mexican hospitality and liquor. Many people spontaneously jumped up to dance to the loud music; others stayed seated to watch the fun—but all were filled with the inescapable joviality. After having a tongue wetter, people chose from multiple restaurants, quiet, romantic lounges, hot live rock music spots, and elegant venues that offered ballroom music complete with an orchestra performing on an open stage, a beautifully polished wooden dance floor, and elegant and swiftly served dining tables. Entertainers prominent in America often appeared in Juárez dinner and dance clubs to provide floorshows or just to enjoy themselves.

Two of the largest US Army and Air Force bases, Fort Bliss Army and Biggs Airforce, were in El Paso, with thousands of soldiers and airmen, many from Germany and other countries, getting sophisticated missile and armaments training. They were all enthusiastic advocates of visiting Juarez. Packs of hundreds filled the main strip streets of Juarez, mostly in the evenings, as they sought music, drinks, and women.

CHAPTER 34

All Shades of Fun

OTHER FREQUENT BUT unpublicized visitors were going to Juárez for one of its most famous offerings: overnight divorces, which were unobtainable in the US. People would arrive in Juárez solely to get what was commonly and widely known as a "quickie divorce"—expensive but, for many, worth it. It was easy to find a storefront sign advertising "*Abogados*" and "*Divorcios*" there.

In 1961, Marilyn Monroe filed for divorce from Arthur Miller, her husband. Actor Richard Burton's wife, Sybil, filed for her divorce through her lawyer in Jalisco, Mexico, after Burton had been in Puerto Vallarta, Mexico, filming the movie *Night of the Iguana*. Quick divorce was prevalent and available to any foreigner who wished to pursue it, and Juárez was the handiest city to do it in. The legal process was eventually eliminated, thus cutting a bite out of the profitable service.

Nothing could stay the flow of revelers from El Paso to Juarez. During the day, both populations crossed the border to shop and visit their families on the opposite side. Juárez also sported huge arenas for bull fighting, part of Mexico's heritage from Spain. It was a hugely advertised event that drew many stateside tourists who, upon attending the brutal event, were mostly repulsed by the gay atmosphere surrounding it.

In bull fighting, the bull is rushed through the opening door of its ringside holding area to appear, stunned, before a massive, shouting crowd. One "bandoleer"—a sharp sword—is shoved into the muscles on each side of its neck to prevent it from thrusting its horns at the bull fighter, which is its only defense, to its full ability.

The bull's agony is long and pitiful; it sweats and frantically tries to fend off charges by the gallantly clad matador with his red cape, which he waves in front of the bull to entice it to attack. The bull lunges forward at the elusive cape, and the matador arches poetically to allow him to pass through the cape in its blind agony and terror as the crowd loudly cheers on the onslaught. After totally fatiguing the enraged, dehydrated, and panicked bull, the matador finally pulls out his long sword and thrusts it through the bull's neck and throat, giving him his last massive pain as he chokes to death on his own blood. The crowd cheers madly, the bull is dragged off the dusty ground, the music revs up, drinks are served, and souvenirs are bought.

After several fights, the crowd disperses and the arena empties. Some leave delighted. Some leave distraught, never to return. Eventually, bull fighting subsided as a sport, but it is still popularly regarded as a romantic endeavor, and the matador remains a popular symbol of Mexican bravery and valor.

After the high stimulation of the fight, much of the crowd looked for down time in one of a profuse number of restaurants in town. The Central Restaurant, which displayed photos of the numerous American movie stars, such as Clark Gable, who had visited and dined there, had a lengthy menu of steak, salad, and side dishes for a low cost that could never be matched in an El Paso eatery, with its higher food and labor costs. The servers were attentive and overly courteous to the customers, which made all diners feel catered to and special, important, and very comfortable. It was certainly one of my favorite diners.

Many El Pasoans and Mexican citizens in the '50s traveled between the cities on open streetcars. It was quick transit that allowed passengers to hop off and on. One popular place to visit was the great Juárez City Market, which offered all things Mexican: sarapes, dishes, hand-painted plant pots (both for the floor and for hanging), indigenous art, statues, religious relics, embroidered table and bed coverings, elaborate candle holders, and all sorts of home décor items. Silver and gold jewelry were plentiful. Children's toys, clothes, and piñatas—generally two-foot-tall papier-mâché figures in the shape of animals or cartoon characters that you filled with candy to be broken by blindfolded children at a party (the piñata was hung openly from a moving rope and children swung wildly at it to be the one who broke the piñata and got first grab at the candy).

Everything was cheap in Juarez. I visited weekly to fill my car with gas for a fraction of the price I paid in El Paso. And Juárez was the party destination—always open, always cheap, totally geared toward American tourists.

Several bottles of any liquor could be bought for the price of one bottle in El Paso, but only two bottles per person could be brought back across the border—a limit that was defeated by a buyer taking several friends with him to carry the bottles across. This errand was always run to stock up on booze for a party, wedding, or any social event, including a funeral.

Women felt safe enough to drive to Juárez from El Paso to get their hair styled lavishly, or to get manicures and pedicures. El Paso men sought out haircuts, hot-towel shaves, and shoe shines there. Cigarettes were bought by the carton, smoking being in broad use at this time (its health risk had yet to be widely exposed). Many people took advantage of lower healthcare costs by visiting dentists or doctors there, although many El Pasoans were also rigidly opposed to getting such professional medical care there as too many stories of ineffective and even harmful procedures—people having teeth filed or replaced by a crown and then losing the teeth, for example—circulated. Seamstresses were available at minimum cost and were proficient at alterations of male and female apparel and at making new garments. Quilting, knitting, and hand-crocheted blankets for babies or large beds was a popularly sought-out home décor purchase.

Juárez was just a fun town where, since the peso was so devalued against the American dollar, the price of most anything was vastly attractive. Many of the nightclubs hosted entertainers from the states or had their own master of ceremonies who presented a variety of floor shows, including singers and dance or comedy routines, usually scheduled every one or two hours, between which dance music was provided.

A place called the Fiesta Club hosted top-notch entertainment and offered elegant dining. The Chinese Palace on the main strip specialized in rowdy, humorous live entertainment, while the Catacombs club, with its low-lit, descending stairway winding down into a seemingly underground area of walls and ceilings made of caves, was a hideaway with a quiet, romantic mood. This was the place for quiet conversation and flirtation while being attended upon by waiters with towel-draped arms hoisting silver serving trays balancing drinks in ornate glassware; its atmosphere was conducive to marriage proposals or plotting criminal activity in privacy. The live hard rock of the Lobby Club, meanwhile, poured through its open doors nightly, pounding the streets with the Long John band's commanding music, which stirred anyone within hearing distance to dance. At Tommy's Rendezvous, a piano player with a repertoire of current songs invited quiet conversation among friends with his crooning voice and agile fingers. People often club hopped between the allure of this multitude of party places, greeting friends in passing and rotating between locations.

The Greyhound dog races and horse races, which ran intermittently, also were crowded events and, during their seasons, were often the main draw for people from both cities of the Rio Grande. Attendees could bet, drink, and socialize in a competitive betting game. Slot machines drew solitary gamblers who had unlimited time to indulge their habit.

The constant flow of customers in the evenings, particularly on weekends, didn't dissipate until dawn, when people started walking or driving or taking cabs across the border back to El Paso.

The tourism into Mexico was far extended past Juarez. Vacation spots in the interior were inexpensive, catered, and beautiful. Cancún, Mazatlan, Acapulco, Zihuatanejo—the oceanfront of which had once been owned by my uncles Benjamin and Pepe—and Puerto Vallarta were frequented beach resort areas.

In 1981, I took my young family to soak up the lavish beach life and entertainment of coastal Mexico. As I sprawled on beach towels on the sand of Puerto Vallarta's ocean, a couple of hang gliding solicitors came up to me and offered to hang glide us. Davy, age eight, was too young to participate, but Tresha (age thirteen) and I ran to the boat as it tossed in the Pacific Ocean's surf at the shore's edge, and they put a separate harness on each of us. A rope was attached to the front center of the harness; a small parachute was attached to the back.

The boat driver began to pull us, both attached to the back of the boat, away from the beach as we walked, then trotted, then ran as the boat gradually picked up speed. As the boat went even faster, it slowly elevated us into the air until we were both airborne with our parachutes fully inflated, cruising above the motorboat at the height of two hundred feet. We flew around the shores of the Pacific for about ten minutes, and then the boat driver skillfully decreased his speed so our parachutes lowered us back down to ground level on the beach, at the same spot from which we had left. As our feet touched the sand, we ran and then walked slowly until we were steadily and firmly back on solid ground, and the boat driver detached our harnesses.

Tresha and I rejoiced in the thrill of that experience. Davy was initially disappointed that he couldn't go too, but he kept himself entertained by following a huge iguana that he spotted roving the beach.

CHAPTER 35

An Economic Jolt on Both Borders

Before NAFTA, the North American Free Trade Agreement, between Mexico, the US, and Canada, was signed in 1992 by President Clinton and approved by George Bush, profuse numbers of Mexican nationals crossed the US–Mexico border daily. Some moved into the interior of the US to seek jobs; a number stayed in El Paso, where they supplied plentiful and extremely low-wage labor in the areas of child care, domestic work (live-in maids), construction, lawn care, road repair, home painting, and auto repair. This created a flourishing economy in El Paso.

NAFTA opened Mexico to the entry of massive US corporations, many of which relocated to Mexico to take advantage of the low wage requirements. This greatly decreased the cheap labor flow into America. The corporations amassed huge fortunes in Mexico, leaving many American workers bereft of income and many former American strongholds of industry abandoned and impoverished. In Mexico, meanwhile, Mexican President Zedillo and Chihuahua Governor Martinez celebrated the huge opening of the new Acer maquiladora industry, which gave thousands of Mexican citizens jobs and annihilated the same number of jobs in El Paso and other US cities. Farrah, Wrangler, and Levi's clothing, and vast numbers of others across our country, followed the exit for self-gain, all closing their doors to workers and moving south to Mexico, eager to take advantage of the rock-bottom wages they could pay to Mexican workers. El Paso was soon thrown into a recession.

The economic flip that resulted from NAFTA is viewed by many as a betrayal of our citizenry. Some Americans steadfastly considered the jobs surge the agreement created in Mexico a bad deal for the US.

Today, outsourcing US jobs has spread throughout the world. This has opened a scramble to recapture the interests and jobs of the US, which is still an emotional tidal wave.

The maquiladora growth benefited Juarez, and many local young women flocked to the maquiladoras for employment at a bit better than the previous wages paid. Even so, Juárez remained a poor city, still catering to the American population.

And then the scenario darkened. An epidemic of young women workers, many of whom had boarded buses from their hometowns and traveled to Juárez for jobs in maquiladoras, mysteriously went missing on the way to or from work. Their bodies started to turn up in desolate areas, savagely mutilated. The numbers became so consistently and increasingly large that the phenomenon garnered national attention in America, with celebrities amassing at the border, demanding an explanation and solution to the onslaught. No clear reason for methods or motive of the slayings was revealed, and people feared, considering the mutilation of the bodies, that organ gathering might be the culprit.

No explanation was ever given, in the end, and coverage of this story was eventually abandoned. But the result was that Juarez—and all of Mexico, really—had become the place not to visit. The cultural interaction between El Paso and Juarez, along with the joyful partying and shopping in Juárez by El Pasoans, was severely disrupted. In the years since, elegant dinner clubs offering mixed drinks, dancing, live entertainment, and security—an attraction that stands above all others—have flourished in El Paso, making the Juárez attraction decline.

As Juárez slept, its sister city, El Paso, soared to life. Massive investments in new infrastructure, businesses, hotels, and business entrepreneurs revived the city from century-old buildings and decadent living and business areas to impressive, new, city-wide renovation, bringing investors from all parts of the country to join the money-making modernization of the old border town formerly known only for its quaint history.

Mexico joined in by moving in. Rich citizens of Mexico bought or built lavish homes in El Paso to take advantage of the safe security provided by the El Paso PD and intimidating presence of one of the most advanced military bases in the US: Fort Bliss. America had its safety system down, and Mexicans crossing over from unsafe and intimidating cities rushed to absorb American culture. Restaurateurs who in

Juárez had long claimed American patronage moved instead to El Paso to serve the same patrons.

El Pasoans had become addicted to the food, music, and party atmosphere of Juárez and demanded its extension into El Paso. Mariachis followed. Now El Paso had it all: the safety of America, and the soul of Mexico.

I was relieved for my friends and family, especially my adult children, to have venues of entertainment in a safe area, knowing that if they were stopped or approached by the El Paso Police they would be in the best and most secure hands of the law.

On May 14, 2018, *USA Today* reported that the Mexican Army patrols would return to Juárez due to a surge in violence across Chihuahua that resulted in the deaths of eight people in the town of Ignacio Zaragoza, including a political candidate, and also included shootings targeting state police in Juárez and Chihuahua. Chihuahua Attorney General Cesar Piniche Espejel said the Mexican military would be part of patrols with local, state, and federal police. The army swarmed into Juárez to attempt to curb or control the cartel-instigated violence occurring randomly throughout Juarez.

According to statistics from the Juárez Mesa de Seguridad y Justicia (the "Security and Justice Board") there was an increase in homicides in Juárez by June 2018 over the 83 committed by June of the previous year; in fact, a staggering 180 homicides were committed by June 2018 in Juarez, 18 of which were committed on a single weekend. "MEXICO MURDERS RISE 16% THIS YEAR" blared the headlines of the *El Paso Times* on July 24, 2018, saying Mexico had again broken its own record for violence. The 15,973 total killings that took place in the country in the first six months of 2018 surpassed the 13,751 killings that took place in the same time frame of 2017. The rate of murder in Juarez, which was predicted to approach that near the level of Brazil and Venezuela by the end of 2018, ultimately far exceeded the expectation and became known as the Murder Capital of the world in 2019 when the February 2019 murder count was 95, a daily average of 3.4 deaths daily.

The United States is, of course, complicit in the drug-related criminal endeavors that take place in Mexico, due to its own citizenry's appetite for dealing in and consuming drugs. Willing participants on the American side of the border buy the drugs produced in Mexico for their own consumption or engage in the distribution and huge financial benefits of illegal drug sales, which perpetuates the problem of cartel violence.

America had our own Masters of Crime: the Mafia. Five boroughs of New York were home to the most incorrigible international crime syndicate, which also paid its way into immunity from apprehension and prosecution. There are always players and there are always payers.

Today, the extreme danger in rural areas and cities of Mexico and South America still motivates large numbers of people to rush the US border for entry. Some are financially able to buy homes and invest in the US, but huge numbers have no money and become an enormous burden on the social services of the US, which they rely upon for food, housing, medical care, and every form of sustenance, sometimes for generations. Many of these arrivals, legal or illegal, provide useful labor for little pay in the US, but in doing so they simultaneously degrade the wages to be earned by American citizens, undercutting earning power with the cheap competition.

The gracious and spirited culture of the Hispanic people should not be demeaned by their displacement due to poverty and life-threatening crime. This is a world phenomenon that begs a solution—one that, unfortunately, does not seem forthcoming. It also cannot be used as a cause to annihilate the US border security and thereby the financial security and prosperity of Americans, however.

Meanwhile, the headlines keep rolling:

> ***4 Officers Killed, 6 Injured in Ambush***
> September 9, 2018: In a drug cartel ambush in a western region of Chihuahua, Mexico, Chihuahua state police officers' vehicles burst into flames when as many as 40 shooters, hiding in the mountains, opened fire on them. The officers were attacked while returning to their base after transporting three detainees to the town of Cuauhtemoc.

"The best predictor of future behavior is past behavior" is a popular maxim cited by Dr. Phil McGraw in one of his self-help books. Thus humankind. Thus the world. Thus the cartels?

I passed that old house again a few days ago—the one I had stopped in at as a cop sixty years ago to change my uniform after getting soaked delivering a baby. I could in a flash see myself sitting at that table with my mom, hearing the "my father, Lloyd, was a great man" story. You never escape your past. It just jumps out now and then and becomes a reality again.

The house was more broken down than before. And I wasn't in a cop car now. I was driving my new Lexus. I had properties in El Paso amply paying my life expenses, as I had contrived to do when I got into commercial real estate.

The neighborhood looked about the same, though some of the houses had been turned into doctors' offices or bars. The population had shifted. The Mexican minority that comprised my youth was now an 85 percent majority.

You'd never know or hear of a crime problem in Juárez by hearing it talked about. El Paso was vibrant with parades, effusively embellished entertainment areas and restaurants, and the same international mix of Juarez–El Paso shoppers and visitors I had seen as a kid. Crime and international issues and conflicts did not affect the binational friendship and kinship of the two cities' populations—which daily traversed the international border to claim their heritage and mingle with their relatives and friends on either side—in the slightest. The only difference I saw was that it was now El Paso that had established and claimed rights to the restaurant, shopping, and party sites. No one mentioned crime epidemics as portrayed on the news, unless they were law enforcement working on the problem.

It was like a mist, that Hispanic culture. It was in the air, filling the atmosphere with congeniality, centuries-old music, and compulsory hospitality to all comers.

The UTEP I'd attended was almost exclusively Anglo but now was about 90 percent Hispanic. Many Anglo families sent their kids to predominantly Anglo colleges out of town or even out of state, causing an eventual population shift of young Anglos to establish their lives in other cities as more Mexican citizens filled the void.

Sure, there were still car thefts, robberies, and barroom fights, but I wasn't involved anymore and didn't miss it. I did miss my dad and his fruit stand every time I swished by this end of town. I even remembered Spotty, standing on those steps and waiting for me. It was like picking up an old photo album and leafing through the pages.

Most of my friends and nearly all my childhood family had died. Even a couple of my own kids—the children my wife and I centered our lives on—had moved away or died. Youth had its thrills and excitement. It held enticing expectations. Now I had contentment and a lack of energy to chase too much. I was glad to see that people are not preoccupied with who's Mexican and who's white in El Paso anymore. That concern polluted people's social life, employment opportunities, and even self-esteem, with the Mexicans being on the low end every time.

I find the new mix is good.

I toast to the Mexican Mix.

If I had to pick a quick few minutes of my life that exemplify the surge or epitome of the thrill of life's essence and joy, I might choose hang gliding over the Pacific Ocean toward the beaches of Mexico's Puerto Vallarta with my little girl, Tresha, hang gliding with me.

EPILOGUE

Winding Down and Exploding—Quick Exits

Patricia

Joe spent eighty-three years in the border town of El Paso, the last thirty-five of which he lived in the first and only house he bought for his family in the center of the city, going daily to his fruit stand. All his kids went to public school within walking distance, and all left home in their late teen years to marry or join the military. His son, David, stayed close to his dad and often went by the house to pick him up and take him to lunch or visited him at his fruit stand, which was always frequented by his dad's lifelong friends, some also from his same area of Mexico.

In the order in which they passed:

Gracie

Joe lived alone in his later years, as Gracie, his wife and companion of over thirty-three years in adventure, family building, and nourishing—through the Depression and war, from the US to Mexico, and back again—had died suddenly at the age of fifty-four, leaving him bereft. He never got to speak to her before she passed in the hospital, surrounded by her grown children, all hoping for her to awaken from whatever had smote her during the night.

Joe

Early one morning, at age eighty-three, as he did his daily stretch exercise before he left for work at his fruit stand downtown, Joe suddenly fell in the bathroom. He was alone in the house but he was soon discovered by a neighbor and rushed to a hospital in an ambulance. He'd had a stroke. As the only telephone system was the solitary black wall phone in each house, each of his kids were notified during the day when they could be reached. When David was contacted, he raced to be by his dad's side, as his dad had always been by his. He was not to see his Jefe conscious again. He stood erect over his bed as other relatives slowly came to share in the ominous and inescapable death they knew they were witnessing.

Ed

My father, Ed Akin, age fifty-nine, got up from his living room chair, from which he was watching an evening TV show (on the then black-and-white-only viewing screen), just a few days after Thanksgiving. He was eating leftover pumpkin pie when he said he had a bad pain. He walked from the living room to the bedroom, where he lay down, never to get up again. He fell unconscious, and didn't awaken.

My mother, Lucy, called a neighbor, who tried to do resuscitation on my father as the ambulance was awaited. I raced with David to meet her at the hospital. She said and seemed assured that nothing serious was wrong, but upon arriving, her first words were, "Dad died."

It was a coronary embolism in the lower back, swift and fatal. It struck down the Akin family rock who built the homes, traveled the roads to Lordsburg and Ruidoso, New Mexico, to sell RCA products, rotating one week at home and one week driving his car to sell merchandise for salary plus commission. He left a fifty-five-year-old wife with no earning potential and Ed's last and youngest child, a sixteen-year-old-daughter, behind. He also, however, left enough life insurance to pay off the well-kept, moderate-income house that he had built when he brought his young family to El Paso, and onto which he had built a third bedroom and extended kitchen. He had laid and cultivated a manicured lawn, willow tree, and garden, and built a wooden dog house with a slanted roof, insulated from winter cold, for his small pet dog in the backyard.

The "keeper" was gone. What would happen to the no longer kept? Ed's social security supported his wife and paid for his last daughter's college education.

The "Keeper" was still keeping.

Lucy

The only one of our parents to not be gifted with a swift exit was the one who'd had a painful early life, having been born to an abusive father who rejected her handicap of a cleft palate, which prevented her from forming words effectively and impeded her speech. It was not the days of swift and advanced child surgeries, so my mother suffered derision throughout her childhood years and was only granted the mercy of surgical treatment—and so freed of the impediment—at the age of sixteen. With the nightly help of an older sister, no speech therapist being available, she practiced saying words properly, and within a year had mastered the task so that no improper inflection was apparent.

Lucy's confidence enhanced, her hidden nature emerged: she was a very social, stylish lady who mastered the Charleston and was an exceptional and gifted dancer. People always said Lucy could "sure carry a tune," meaning she had a good singing voice, and she often sang "Saint Louie Women," which was popular in her young days. She was loved by her family for her devotion and care of her four children, all of whom she sent to Catholic Elementary school, as well as Confession on Friday and Mass on Sunday, though she said in her later years that religion had ruined her life. Loved by her neighbors, sisters, aunts, and cousins, all of whom were entertained by her sense of humor through it all, she began in her late fifties to down a couple evening glasses of wine to assuage life's turmoil.

When my father died, my mother joined a social group called "Parents Without Partners," met many friends, and remarried within a few years. She had heart surgery at the age of seventy-five and suffered increasingly poor health afterward. In her last year of life, she was placed into a private nursing home by her second husband, and put into hospice. She suffered long-term anxiety and dementia over two years before she died at age eighty-one, struggling for breath. The Grim Reaper had tortured her, the most deserving of a peaceful death.

Thoughts of Mom

I wish I could be back in Mom's warm kitchen,
With the noise, turmoil and dissension,
I thought that was my forever.
But now it is my never.
—*Patricia, 2019*

Perspectives and Poetry of Patricia Rodriguez

Our firstborn: Patrice, born July 29, 1964, died May 26, 2009

Thus Ends

Thus ends the experience of Patrice. It also ends her beautiful brown eyes, sculpted nose, full and perfectly shaped lips, classic bone structure, and once-exquisite figure. It ends her great laugh, non-judgmental acceptance of everyone, and love of every animal ever born, especially Kujo and Midget, her pet dogs who slept next to her. It ends her queries—"Isn't Nicole beautiful?"; "Is she happy in college?"; "How's my little bro, David? When's he fighting again? I'm going to go, so be sure to let me know"; "What's 'Twisted' Tresha doing?"; and "How's my dad, is he okay?"

Patrice had an all-forgiving, great, loving heart and ready sense of humor, and therefore lots of friends in her life. She partied a lot. She fell in love—not wisely, but with vigor.

She dressed up, looked gorgeous, laughed, and enjoyed. She also felt disillusioned, sad, and cried.

In grade school and high school, Patrice was a friend to any underdog or kid in her class who was generally ignored by others. People just liked her. She was a talented writer, and she created and put on plays in our backyard and at neighbors' houses, giving kids lines and roles; she was the source of her sister, Tresha's, love of acting. She was an equestrian and became a skilled rider in her early teen years. Caring for and training horses was her most loved hobby during her young years.

Patrice also grappled with depression, discontent, and turmoil in her life, but meant no harm to anyone and always grieved her mistakes.

She had a soft and sweet side. No one was crazy for holidays like Patrice; her favorites were decorating and making treats and chili bowls for Halloween parties, hanging lights all over her apartment on Christmas, and blasting off firecrackers in the desert on the Fourth of July. She loved her daughter, Nicole, and all of her family, most of all.

Next, she loved lobster.

Whatever imbalances we saw in Patrice's life, we saw a huge, loving heart thumping all through it, and we loved her right back.

A Concert

We went to a concert, Elton John
Her eyes sparkling and shiny
She swooned into a distant space
With an entranced smile on her glowing face
Tantalizing friendly drugs brought
The excitement and ecstasy she sought.

Auditorium crushingly packed
Other fans with a bottle sacked
I worried, in her fragile state
How, in a crowd surge,
Could I get her out the gate?

Her rhythmic sway, her sense of surroundings did deaden
As she lived and loved her own pure heaven
I'm glad I saw her sublime spirit
A respite from her ever pain
The music; my heart will forever hear it
My mind sits by and watches her, again and again.

Patrice and Me

Patrice is not lost to me,
She just liked to be free.
Her beauty, warmth, humor, laughter,
I'll always love and see.
Sparkling, brown, enchanting eyes,
Sculpted beautiful face.
Had a zest for biker guys,
Racy parties and Levi's.
A magnet for friends and men,
Dread when the party must end.
Cruising on the fun of life,
Got some slams and blows,
Suffered hurts and strife.
How deep within her soul
My real Patrice resides,
No one can know, but
There my little girl hides.
Her childhood is her memory's
Safe ground. Warmth, love, parties,
Conjure a secure jovial sound.
Piñatas, Xmas trees, movies,
Disneyland, Snoopy,
French Provincial bedroom set,
Her future a safe bet.
Then teenage years and the rush to roam.
Now her mind can dip into that child's past,
Close her eyes and step right in.
The door, the hallway,
The room that has been,
Stays perfectly intact,
For comfort, to come back.

A Dad

He is underlying sad
Laughs, but not uproariously
Like he had
Two bits, four bits, six bits, a daughter.
Gave forty-four years doing all
He thought he "oughter"
Her life trail twisted his head and heart
With soul-breaking wrench
Nothing he advised, pleaded, promised
Devised, extinguished her thirst
Or damaged his love.

Soft, beautiful, vulnerable brown eyes
Her former sunshine in dynamic bursts
Over years resigned, "I'm gone, Dad" sighs.

He sees her lie there, soon she'll die
No more weapons has this gladiator
To make it pass by
Longer years of hope,
Bartering with her soul

Appears the Reaper to claim his meager dole
Sucks out her life and her dad
Into a black hole.

Chasing Patrice

The cosmos, dust, planets and stars,
I can't find your place
Don't know where you are.
You went in the night, so fast, so far.

When my body dies,
Will I rise? Will I see your
Spiritual beautiful face,
Will joy come then and all pain erase?

Our love clings to you
Chasing your path. Where can you be?
Can you come back?

Wildly we try to connect with you
To say good bye and assure you
Of the great, deep love surrounding
Patrice-e-Boo

We grieve, cry, and ask why.
You were from God a great gift.
Did we not help you?
Not give your spirits a lift?
We crave you in our eternal love,
Please be at peace in the somewhere above.
—*May 2009*

DESERTED DAD

I no longer recognize that man out there,
With the slicked back grey and black thick hair,
And grooved, disinterested, lusterless face.

Like he has no more zest, or things to chase.
He sprays the lawn as his mind wanders
To a time with a baby girl, his feet always under,
Or on his broad shoulders bore,
For a fast run to a candy store.

Forty-four years later he visits some planet,
Where she plays in his memory, that cannot wane,
He covets and yearns for the child,
Killed in adulthood by life with the wild.

He broodingly speaks to her as grown, in his mind,
Assures her he loves her and no fault can he find,
With her tortured life and slip-away death,
That left him sobbing in each breath.

He sees her again, running through the water hose,
Frozen in a giggling, three-year-old pose.
—June 2009

Running from Patrice

After grieving, sobbing, talking,
You left us nothing to say.
We've tried to unthread
What happened to you, day and night and day.

Tired, somber, quiet, fruitless, numb,
Our immersion into sorrow
Gives us a zero sum.

When flashes of your happy or dying face
Invade our murky minds,
We push it back to erase, so peace in life we may find.

To let go, live, and breathe without pain,
We must forget you again.
—*July 2009*

The Deadness of Patrice

The feeling now is stale and glum
Sometimes the feeling doesn't even come
With brief tranquility a stab interferes
Her face or laugh moves close, hurls the spear

I sink a bit and a memory grab,
Then rush hurriedly into life's frantic swirl
I do not reflect on the little girl,
Or her whole life of enigma and pain
Which would drag me to destruction, not gain.

I hold a hard line here,
Against one for whom
I once would have died,
And for many tears cried.
Desperate passionate years warding her
Away from danger, offering her the best,
I hadn't the answer so failed the test.

After age thirteen, over the next thirty years
She became more a stranger;
Abstract sick, sweet, hostile,
But interspersing "I love you Mom."
With a soft, beautiful smile.

When she pops into my channel,
I turn the dial.
Hoping not to confront her life forever;
Or for a long while.

So far I've outrun her except for a sudden
Feeling, or a bizarre dream. Such is my scheme,
I hope to go so fast,
She'll mercifully get stuck in the past.
—*September 2009*

And Now, One Year Later, Our Patrice

You've left us the remnants
We try to get by on them.
The void can't fill
It misses the gem.
Your sparkling eyes
Blind as we advise.

Now you see; you tell us so
By contact, counsel, signs,
Shared insights
A consoling glow.

We know you're in our sphere
Now the one who's wise
We feel you there
You touch us here
Holding each other dear.
—*May 2016*

The Outback

As close as yesterday, as far as never
When I'll see her as I saw her last
Not ever.
I feel her hug me, "Bye Mom,"
Hear her tell me on the phone what she's cooked.
I see every pore of her skin,
Sparkling brown eyes
Beautiful sculpted face
Laugh and luster gone away
I hear her flat chat of mundane things
And I say "I have to go now."
"Okay Mom." In my heart it rings
Did she wonder, "Doesn't she know?"

Pulling her from cliff's edge
Thirty years of adulthood
Obliterated most of her image as a girl,
So good and giving a caretaker of others
Whatever stage of her I reach
I hear and see myself
Chase, plead, bargain and preach

I fear diminishing clarity of memory
As I lose hold and she fades to the never
Will I suddenly sharply panic
To close the breach?
Can I stop pursuing, cease my reach?
Will she always hover?
Does she know I love her?
Is she still real?
Deserted Dad

She gave me signs: a Queen of Hearts
She showed me a hot yellow giraffe
I can see but not quite hear her voice
Further from me she departs
Can she not stir in my soul
Some feeling, more signs to console?

Yesterday moves away, leaves no choice
I stare into the never; stark
One light I pray Patrice, one light in my dark.
—*August 2016*

Tresha, My Forever Friend

I have a great love who lives apart from me.
Her beautiful face, champagne laugh, sparkling hair,
Elegant gait
I vividly see.

Daily the phone nourishes our broad spectrum of thoughts,
Conversation, understanding, hurts and humor.
We throw in truth, wishes, plans, books, and rumor.
My soul connected spirit, and precious gift,

A dazzling light through a heavenly shaft,
Her absence a hole, a lonely draft.
On this downside of a speeding roller coaster,
Before I get off, I just want to toast her.

Her little toys, grown boys,
Theatre, travel, dance and joys,
Are seared into my soul.
A mother holding every minute of her life
As precious memories in a sacred bowl.
—*September 2009*

David, My Son

Strong heart, razor sharp,
Loves deep, friends everywhere.
Always loyal. Share and care.
Gorgeous, outrageous.
Champion hitter, WINNER.
Women spinner.
Rigor, vigor, pull the trigger.
Everything hot, got to rock.
Dynamic, tough, rough.

Precious baby, twisting my hair twixt his fingers,
So in his sleep I'd stay,
Telling him stories, and not slip away.
Handsome, loving, unrestrained, exploring child,
Pitching tents, climbing mountains, fishing,
Catching hermit crabs, lizards, love for the wild.
I taught him to read and pray,
"I love you," as I hugged him he'd say.
Then race to capture the fun in his day

All this from where?
A star explosion way out there?
He fills all lives with zest.
I've been given the number one best.

Mothers get the impact, the fallout.
His presence in my heart he cannot rout.
Mom's love is deep forever, no conditions, no doubt.
My son David is my sun.
—September 18, 1997

My Nicole: My Special Gift

A soul soaring lift, a thrill, a joy,
To hold, smell, and kiss, my new God's gift.
Beauty of soul, my Nicole,
Beauty of face to compel,
Love's eternal spell.

How had I achieved such unearned grace,
To have her fall into my arms, my life, my space.
Sculpted elegant features,
Nature's lovely creature.

Tiptoed through stickers,
Stepped onto satin cushions,
Flown on angel wings through strife: a joyous dancer,
The essence of good, by choice, not chance.

Blesses me with daily calls. We talk with solid trust.
We share our fun and troubles, trading advice, a must.
A sweet, honest child and friend,
As loyal confidants, we blend.
Her glow allows others to shine.
I so love this precious gift of mine.
—January 7, 2002

Written for My Son: As You Step

Actually,

Everything in life you do leaves a footprint on someone's heart, soul, personality, view of life, self-esteem, or hopes, as well as on your own.

Your steps by the minute, in life, sear through everyone around you, or far off, who hear of, or see your steps, like energy zapping as it passes. The very same energy and effect of your steps equally invade you, reinforcing, reinventing, or regressing your own knowledge or resolve. Steps boost or diminish your spirit, your temple of God: your mind, body and soul.

Watch your steps, measure each one. Step on no one's heart or face. Use your steps to lead, showing a way others admire, emulate, or at least feel good about the fallout you generate. Step on a right path; you may never be able to erase imprints you've made with careless, cruel missteps.

Step with purpose, love, and positivism, deep breathing and focused on your creator. Do not create trash; create empowerment in people. Lead by example; do not slump along like an undirected mishap. Know what you're doing, after getting the best counsel in every situation.

Then step with power, pride, and calmness of heart, all of which you give yourself,

By the steps you take.
—*March 2008*

The Journey

To my son, David Nino, with great admiration and love.

You've taken many beautiful steps in life.

You stepped into the ring with passion and courage, dominating it for twenty years. You stepped into hospital sick children's rooms with encouragement and uplifting spirit.

You stepped away from physical mutilation and death, with stunning pain, pushing away fear, anguish, and loss of hope.

You stepped into crowded auditoriums of timid, rowdy, troubled children, to sooth and compel them with fiery, compassionate and dynamic oratory of your life's trauma and bliss, giving faith and direction.

You stepped into planes to see God's world: peaks of Mayan pyramids where ancestors meditated in worship seeking the great spirit, into Australian Outbacks of dispirited populace, filling their hunger on kangaroos, into Rome's Coliseums, whispering of gladiators and chariots, into Mexico's music and murder, into New York's frantic bustle, Amsterdam's laxity, and ancient Greece's Spartans and Parthenon of philosophers.

You splashed the world with your book. One month was all it took.

Switch and turn; ice and burn, you told it the way you lived it.

So many people have felt the thunder and the softness of your steps.

Marked impressions on the sands of thought,
So freely shared, so dearly bought.
Your heart is ready for what your soul has sought,
Your feet are shod for The Journey.
—2017

My Husband: What I Most Admire

Dynamic personality, aggressive zest for life, combined with casual down-to-earth friendliness, a hearty laugh and sense of humor, attracting friends without effort. His extensive immersion into the cultures of the Orient, the Pacific Islands, Europe, Mexico, South America, Canada, in addition to five years as a policeman and detective in Narcotics and Bunco all provided an intense exposure to elements of crime, adventure and human frailty. He is non-judgmental, like his dad. Handsome, a muscular six-foot-three with square jaw, hazel eyes, and a smile flashing perfect white teeth. Innovative, building his own real estate business into significant ownership of properties and money, a motorcycle rider and hang glider, highly competitive in poker and sports. A passionate lover and untiring counselor of his children. An advocate and fan of football and basketball. A man's man. A woman's man. All man. A sharpshooter and a straight shooter; the answer to any young woman's illusions or dreams. If my husband should precede me in the final journey to the next dimension, and I should try to conjure a glimpse of him there, I think I would see him on his blazing red motorcycle, heading for a poker game.

My Children's Vision

I pray that in my children's hindsight vision, they will remember Thanksgiving dinners, Christmas mornings, an always beautifully set table, family laughter, crowds of friends, parties, bands, singers, belly dancers, children's choir, lights and music, with Dad's booming laughter and Mom's energetic joy, always overseeing this vacationing, gregarious, devoted family culture.

Can they recapture the feelings of warmth, and camaraderie so spontaneous and rich? Can they trip back in time, be there again, like the turning of a switch?

WE ARE ALL TRAVELERS
ADIEU

Always

About the Author

PATRICIA RODRIGUEZ has a bachelor's degree in education. A teacher of twenty-five years, she is also a travel, dance, and history enthusiast.

About the Contributing Author

DAVID F. RODRIGUEZ is a college graduate, athlete, traveler, sailor, policeman/detective, real estate acquisitionist, and world explorer.